STUCK ON THE CUBS

By Rick Schwab

SASSAFRAS PRESS
Evanston, Illinois

Published by Sassafras Press, Inc
August, 1977

Library of Congress Catalog Card Number: 77-83921
ISBN: 0-930528-01-8
Cover Photograph by Steven Schwab

TO A FUTURE CUB FAN

Danny Schwab, age three months

PRINTED IN THE UNITED STATES OF AMERICA

Acknowledgments

MARK EISENSTEIN (Brewer Fan)

Thanks for nodding with approval no matter what junk I test-read to you.

GLORIA JOSEPH (Bull Fan)

Thanks for deciphering my scribble and typing my scrambled thoughts.

HEIDI LEVIN (Pirate Fan)

Thanks for correcting my punctuation and for your cryptic remarks. In case we left out some punctuation, following is a line of marks to scatter about: ?”“.,:,“:;;!!,;:“//;/“???’ “::;.,:?:/

ROBERT LEWIN (White Sox Fan: Luigi)

Thanks for showing me what dopes White Sox fans are and thereby convincing me to be a Cub fan.

DEBBIE LINKOWSKI (Sox Fan)

Thanks for stifling your partisanship and not sabotaging the book while you typed it.

MELINDA METZGER (Cub Fan)

Thanks for spending six hours with me in the bleachers gathering statistics for the Appendix and giggling at some of the averages.

NANCY PHILIPPI (Not a Fan)

Thanks for editing this book from 400 pages to 200 pages. You turned me from a wit to a half-wit.

DIANE SCHWAB (Exchange National Bank Fan)
Thanks for cooking for me, putting up with my eccentric moods and schedules, and for saving my money.

HANK SCHWAB (Father of Cub Fans)
Thanks for writing my best stories and watching the store.

STEVEN SCHWAB (Cub Fan)
The brains behind the operation. He wheeled and dealed like a precinct captain with an opening in the Department of Streets and Sanitation.

KAY SILVER (N.U. Wildcat Fan)
Thanks for being the first to read the completed manuscript and telling me "Hey, it was really mediocre."

JEFFERY A. SMITH (Benton Ranger Fan)
Thanks for compiling hours of statistics (none of which we used) and for discussing story ideas over endless pizzas.

Table of Contents

FOREWORD

In his farewell address to his fans in Yankee Stadium, Babe Ruth stated, in his cancer-stricken voice, already reduced to a whisper, "Baseball is the greatest game in the world." Damn it, I believe him. Of course, Babe Ruth was a person of such magnitude and forthrightness that had he said, "Mumbly-Peg is the greatest game in the world," switchblades would be up ten points on the stock market.

But anyone who has felt the solid connection of bat on ball, anyone who has raced frantically toward a base and then sprawled recklessly into the bag a fraction of a second ahead of a desperate tag, anyone who has sped toward that falling white sphere in the sky, extended arm to its fullest capacity, and then felt the contact between ball and glove, anyone who knows the exhilaration of stepping up to the plate in the most pressure-packed part of the game and then lining the ball into the left field corner, knows baseball is the greatest game in the world.

You don't even have to have played baseball. Love for the game comes merely from hearing the crack of the bat on a sundrenched spring day. It comes from a balmy breeze tickling your neck at the open collar, from watching the graceful athletes with the deeply imbedded bronze tans glide across the dark green of the outfield, from the holiday spirit at home on the day your family has tickets for the Sunday doubleheader, from the look in your boy's eye after he received a wink and an autograph from his favorite player, but most of all from that wildly hysterical feeling you get when a hopeless situation is averted because a lightly regarded pinchhitter smacks one across the street. The captivating power of baseball can best be seen everyday in the stands, when otherwise quiet and colorless people leap on their seats, arms swinging insanely over their heads, strange shrieks of joy emitting from their throats.

No other sport can match baseball for its frequently dramatic, bizzare denouement. In hockey, football and basketball, there is a point where it is humanly impossible to catch up because of the time element in these sports. In baseball, as long as the game is not officially over, there's always time to beat the opponent.

What I have said may not convince everyone that baseball is the greatest game in the world. Backgammon fans will still think they have the best game, the curling advocates will not come over, and even croquet will still have its supporters. But, I am a militant baseball man, and only begrudgingly give permission for sports fans of all idealogies to read this book.

Baseball and the Cubs have been my religion for twenty years. I have missed hearing or seeing very few ball games in their entirety during this span. Day after day, I have scanned the sports pages for comments on the Cubs, talked baseball with casual acquaintances during the day, watched the ballgame, read the evening paper for more information, and watched the ten o'clock news for the latest baseball happening. Frankly, though,

I've found the newscasts and reporting trite, boring, repetitious, and unoriginal for the most part. You know the comments: "He puts out 125 percent for you." "He has all the tools." "He can fly."

The most entertaining sports information can be found at the tavern where true and often knowledgeable sports' fans gather and exchange opinions. Here's where the lively comments and conjecture are heard. The fans should write the newspaper articles. They don't have to stay on good terms with the big egos on the ballclub and are free to give unbiased, direct opinion of the events. They are the ones who should comment publicly on the Cubs. Carrying it one step further, I am a fan and have a journalism degree to boot. No one has better credentials to write the story of the Cubs than I.

This book has been swimming through my mind for some time. There have been many sports books written, but few, if any, were from the fan's viewpoint. There have been books such as Jim Brosnan's *The Long Season,* or Jerry Kramer's *Instant Replay* in which the season's unfolding was told from the player's perspective.

This book is written for the fans by a fan. Now sit back with a drink, put your feet up, and pretend we're at the bar discussing Jose Cardenal's latest antic ....

Dear Cubbie Fans:

We are a unique lot. I hesitate to call us a minority. With the possible exception of the New York Yankees and the Los Angeles Dodgers, the Cubs have more fans than any other team in America. There are tens of thousands of transplanted Chicagoans around the country who have spread the gospel; people who have worked, gone to school, passed through, or visited in Chicago. Ernie Banks, Mr. Cub, is one of the most popular ballplayers in the history of baseball. Most of all, the Cubs have been a loser since World War II and everybody loves a loser.

I have met Cub fans in Europe, in California, in Georgia, and even on the south side of Chicago. When two Cub fans meet, tears well in their eyes. Without saying a word, both parties know the torment the other has endured for 32 years. Nothing need be said about the 19-2 shellackings the Cub pitchers designed. Or the endless near suicide-provoking bottom-of-the-ninth losses on the road. Or the 3-2 squeakers where the Cubs just couldn't get the big hit when their breathtaking game-winning rally (bases loaded-nobody out) flopped, leaving that loathsome taste in the mouth.

There is no getting around the monumental record of ineptitude the Cubs have methodically carved. Over half the nation was born after World War II and none of them have ever seen the Cubs win a pennant. There are over 100 professional sports teams in our country, and none of them can approach the folly that is the Cubs. Yet, shallow-brained loyalists continue to support the Cubs year after year through the thin and the thin. Why do Cub fans persevere?

We are victims of the media; victims of a massive propaganda program not seen since the Third Reich. Chicago has gathered the most unrealistic collection of sportswriters and commentators conceivable. I'm not saying these guys are doltish (although recently a very, very long-time announcer of Cub games suggested that a batter might be given the take sign with two strikes on him), but their opinions, which are force fed to Cub fans, are mush.

Winning attitudes help championship teams to win. Similarly, fans must accept and be told the truth (this does not mean Cub fans have to admit a damn thing to Sox fans) so that they can figure out what's happening and put pressure on the management to deliver what is lacking. For years, announcers have been telling us Cub players can do no wrong. Low average hitters were always hitting in bad luck. Cub pitchers never threw at the opposition, the pitch just got away from them. And the sportswriters have always been too slow to criticize and too quick to praise. A Cub relief pitcher who has been a marginal performer for five years has a hot two months and the scribes write about the impregnability of the bullpen. Baloney!

There is a difference between soggy-brained optimism and a winning attitude. The media's failure in being hard-nosed lulls the fans into contentment with losing teams. Because the Cubs pander to the media, they are treated like mama's little baby. The commentators who implore the

Cubs to win two out of three in an upcoming series (as if a sweep would be too selfish despite 32 years of being the sweepee) do not help the Cubs. Neither do those who insist on asking, "Are the Cubs for real?" instead of adopting the philosophy, "Damn right they are until someone beats them."

It is now time for the rise of a new, militant Cub fan. A fan who will not only abhor defeat but will reject the ignominy of being soft-sold the defeat by the sugar-coating media.

It is not easy to turn a soft, cubby bear into a grizzly overnight. Sometimes people have to be hit over the head before they will wake up. Therefore, I have regurgitated my own 25 years as a Cub fan in the hopes that seeing how crazy we've all been to put up with a loser all these years will unite us to push for excellence.

DAMN IT, WE DESERVE A WINNER.

My childhood years were traumatic ones. I was raised in White Sox country. A cub fan fares on the south side of Chicago like an Arab living in Israel.

My first inclination was to stifle my patriotism and go along with the program in my neighborhood. After all, this was in the 50's before black pride, women's lib and gay rights. If the Cubs won a game with a homer in the ninth, I figured I could join the others in the closet to scream with joy.

But two things gradually became apparent to me. First, I noticed a few oddballs who flagrantly cheered Roy Smalley Sr. when his throws from shortstop arrived in the first baseman's glove and not in the first base box seats. These same fans exulted in White Sox defeats. I could see there was room for the loyal opposition.

Additionally, I discovered that when the Sox won, I felt sick. The droning monotone of Bob Elson reporting on the Sox 1-0 victory as Sherman Lollar's sacrifice fly drives in Jim Rivera who had been hit by a pitch, bunted over to second, and balked to third, caused the original Excedrin headache number 1. And when Ferris Fain hit one of the six homers he produced in the 1953 season and I heard Elson say, "A White Owl Wallop and a box of White Owl Cigars", God, I hated White Owl Cigars even more than when I finally smoked one.

The Sox are a lacklustre, anemic, pesky conglomerate of near athletes. They are to baseball what George Gobel is to the entertainment world, limited talent and boring.

And it doesn't take long to get annoyed at the Sox victories over the likes of the St. Louis Browns, Washington Senators, Seattle Pilots and Mariners, Kansas City A's and the other watered down opposition the American League offers.

Occasionally you will hear one of our empty-headed aldermen mumble how wunnerful it would be for the city of Chicago if both teams do well.

No self respecting Cub or Sox fan will ever wish the other team well. Cub and Sox fans are natural enemies who maybe wouldn't go as far as rooting for a plane crash but sure would relish a flat tire on the runway.

Cub fans smile at Sox losses, at Sox attendance figures, at tornados on Sox home dates, at the quality of food at Sox park, at the Sox scoreboard mis-firing, at Sox singers who forget words of the national anthem, at Bill Veeck's Mexican Fiesta Day, and are absolutely regaled with laughter when the Sox lose a doubleheader.

Sox fans get hysterical when they think of the Cubs record since 1945 and the 1969 season in particular.

Nothing was as funny for Sox-lovers as 1969.

Lament of the frustrated Cub Fan:

"The Cubs will be alive in '75"
"The Cubs will give us kicks in '76"
"The Cubs will put us in heaven in '77"

Please don't even bother to tell me what they will be in '78; I couldn't stand the agony. Even the (pardon the expression) White Sox had their place in the sun when the sirens went off all over the city in 1959. When you look at the last time the Cubs won, in 1945, that doesn't seem like yesterday.

I remember it well — the radio blaring loudly while Mom changed my diapers. But please, God, couldn't we have just one more pennant for our Northsiders before I die of old age? Please?

I can see that our country runs on publicity — PR as the "professionals" call it. Okay, so they have to say things that aren't necessarily 100 percent true in order to get people interested in products or movie stars or candidates for election, but do they have to tamper with my Cubs and tell me how great they are, year after year, month after month, day after day and then cheat me, in '73, in '74, in '75, in '76, etc., etc., out of that pennant that I so richly deserve?

The state of mind I'm in now, why I can just imagine seeing the schedule for 1978 in the paper: yes, here it is: Opening Day, April 6: New York Mets vs. Pittsburgh Pirates at Pittsburgh; Philadelphia Phillies vs. Fairbanks Cubs at Fairbanks,

Alaska ... yes, Fairbanks, Alaska. If the Cubs don't win this year, I couldn't care less. If nobody in Fairbanks wants the Cubs, maybe Hattiesburg, Mississippi could use them — just get them out of my hair. See if I give a hoot. I've had it. I'll be a Bull fan. I'll love the Blackhawks. Even the Bears. You see, I am glad when they win but when they lose, I don't get that upset. But the Cubs, the Roller Coaster Cubs with their hills and their valleys, they make me sick. They can go to H-----attiesburg.

I take it all back. I want the Cubs in Chicago on Opening Day in 1978. After all, I'm stuck on the Cubs: "The Cubs will be great in '78."

Cub fans wear rose colored glasses. This explains why the Cub management has been able to present 32 consecutive annual editions of has beens, never wases, potential has beens and potential never wases, without summer riots.

Some of us were thinking of forming the Cub Fan Defense League to prevent the reoccurrence of atrocities such as in 1969, but we couldn't find a fan with an IQ over 90 to organize it.

We are quick to ridicule errors by the New York Mets or inept .222 hitters on the Houston Astros, but should they have the Cubby bear emblem on the left shoulder of their uniforms, we malign the condition of the field or get hot about allowing spit ball pitchers to operate.

The Cubs in my lifetime have not understood how to play ball. Their teams have been loaded with slow-footed, Wrigley Field-only power hitters, who beam with satisfaction when they make it to first base and are so enamored with being on base at all that they never make it to second. (Cub runners have to be urged to advance more than one base on home runs.) They think "playing the field" means dating several girls at once. The significance of pitching has eluded the Cub braintrust. They always looked on it like a lottery ... if one body on the mound isn't doing it, bring in another; maybe he'll have more luck. Strategy has been non-existent. The Cubs grew up on tiddly winks, not war games. Yet Cub fans still get awe-struck by a routine fly ball to left. They are easily impressed and rarely get on their players unless they show a cocky streak as did Ron Santo.

Cub fans and management are not the keenest judges of talent. If they were, how could players such as Preston Ward, Bill Serena, Chuck Connors, Gene Hermanski, Bob Ramazotti, Toby Atwell, Bob Addis, Warren Hacker, Clyde McCullough, Joe Garagiola, Bubba Church, Jim King, Bob Speake, Jim Bolger, Pete Whisenant, Hobie Landrith, Solly Drake, Harry Chiti, Don Kaiser, Vito Valentinetti, Jim Brosnan, Cal Neeman, Dave Hillman, Dick Drott, Sammy Taylor, Johnny Goryl, Taylor T-Bone Phillips, Bill Henry, Bob Anderson, Ed Bouchee, Elvin Tappe, Seth Morehead, Al Heist, Dick Bertell, Jackie Curtis, Don Landrum, Cal Koonce, Ellis Burton, Paul Toth, Len Gabrielson, Billy Cowan, Jimmy Stewart, Vic Roznovsky, Robert Pena, Chris Krug, Bill Faul, Adolfo Phillips, Bryon Browns, John Boccabella, Bob Hendley, Ted Savage, Ray Culp and a cast of thousands have participated in Cub lore during my tenure as a fan?

Apparently Cub scouts thought most of the above players had all the tools. Maybe they should have become carpenters.

The Del Prado Hotel in the Hyde Park area used to be one of the most plush hotels in Chicago. In recent years, it has been converted into an apartment/hotel set-up, and deterioration has been substantial. There are probably some rats on the waiting list to get into the place.

I spent many summers hanging around the Del Prado hoping to get an autograph or a glimpse of one of the ballplayers from visiting American League teams who stayed there. It was on the lake and only about ten minutes from Comiskey Park.

I was nine years old when I befriended the Boston Red Sox. This was my pre-paunch era and I had a pretty good physique when I inhaled. I was standing in front of the hotel waiting for the players to file out en route to the team bus doing my Tarzan routine when Dick Gernert, Frank Sullivan, and Willard Nixon of the 1955 Bosox came out of the hotel to see me pummeling my friend Luigi (who to this day persists on being a White Sox fan).

The Red Sox watched in amazement as I beat the president of the Dick Donovan fan club senseless, and insisted that I come on the team bus and play Tarzan for the rest of their teammates. This was fine with me since during all the hubbub, Norm Zauchin, who was off to a fantastic start in 1955, and for whose autograph I had been waiting, had already boarded the bus. Norm petered out to

.239 at the end of the year although he did have his best season by far (27 H.R./93 RBI). But in June, 1955 he was an up and coming star. He was 26 years old then and people were saying in ten years he had a chance to be 36. Frank Sullivan and I worked out a deal. He would see that I got Zauchin's autograph if I would make an ass of myself with the Tarzan bit. I agreed. Sullivan was six foot seven inches. It's hard for someone four foot eight to say no to someone six foot seven. The Red Sox got their jollies and I got Zauchin's autograph. He seemed very uncomfortable getting the star treatment; it was as if he knew midnight was coming and he would again turn into a Triple A pumpkin.

The only disappointment of the day was that Ted Williams was not on the bus. The story is that Williams would always get to the park early for extra batting practice, but after meeting his teammates, I figured he couldn't stand those ten minute bus trips.

My next favorite memory was when my brother Steve was 14 and approached Mickey Mantle for his autograph. Mantle pushed my brother to the ground and called him a "fucken asshole". I agreed with Mantle later when I unintentionally locked us out of our house the day of the All Star game and Steve beat me to a pulp.

The day after Mantle had been so kind to Steve, I tried to get his valued signature. Again he strode briskly by the young autograph seekers, but apparently he was in a much more benevolent mood since he didn't shove any ten year olds. He boarded the bus and took a seat by the window. I tapped on his window and reached up with a pen and a hard ball. To my surprise, he opened his window, signed the ball and then proceeded to fire the ball onto the pavement, causing it to bounce up to the second floor window of the hotel. What a gracious guy!

I also met Connie Mack, Casey Stengel, and Al Kaline as an 18 year old rookie at the Del Prado. I work only two blocks from the hotel and pass it every day, but can not do so without thoughts of those great moments of my childhood.

Anchored down with the dehumanizing equipment which must be worn as protection against crippling injuries, the catcher's job is the toughest. He is a fortress guarding the plate as if a crown jewel. He is the stabilizing force on the field serving as father, friend, confidante, and con man to the pitching staff. He is the signal caller, the quarterback. On the Cubs during our endless drought, he has been more like a hunchback.

For some reason, the Cubs have collected the most ludicrous assemblage of pseudo-major leaguers at this key position than any other. Mind you, the other positions haven't been supermen, but thinking of Cub second basemen doesn't necessarily create hysteria. Cub catchers are and always have been jokes.

They come in all shapes and sizes and ethnic origins. We've had tall catchers, such as 6'4" Chris Krug (lifetime .203); fat catchers, like 220 pound Harry Chiti (lifetime .238); small catchers, like 5'9½" Toby Atwell (lifetime .260); skinny catchers, like 170 pound Hobie Landrith (lifetime .233). We've had Polish catchers like Vic Roznovsky (lifetime .217), Mexican catchers like Cuno Barragan (lifetime .202), Italian catchers like Joe Garagiola (lifetime .257), and black catchers like Elrod Hendricks (lifetime .217).

My own darling (if a .238 hitter can be a darling) was Harry Chiti. Besides looking and playing like a buffoon, Harry's last name made him an easy mark. Fans would yell, "Hey, Shitty, when are you going to get a hit?" Chiti never could come back with a nifty rejoinder because it sure beat the hell out of him when he was going to get a hit.

I'm being unkind. I recollect a big hit Harry got. For some inexplicable reason, the opposition was giving Harry an intentional base on balls, a free ride to first (and people are complaining about welfare programs). Perhaps Chiti didn't recognize the intentional walk, perhaps the Cubs had a hit and run on (only the Cubs would do that), as Harry watched the soft lob go by outside for ball one. Another lob outside for ball two. As the pitcher wound up again and threw, images of playing hardball on the corner lot in Kincaid, Illinois as a kid or the time he impressed his date at the church picnic must have conjured in his mind. He sprang at the gently thrown pitch and hit one high and far and on the catwalk ... a home run. The fans stood as one (there was a very small crowd) and screamed. Chiti circled the bases grinning uncontrollably. One fan said it for us all as he stood up and yelled, "Hey, Shitty. That was a stupid thing to do."

Another favorite was .224 lifetime slugger, Cal Neeman. I shouldn't knock Cal since he once gave me a baseball. I used to arrive at the ballpark at 9:30 in the morning so that I could get a front row seat in the bleachers. The reason for a front row seat is to catch a baseball, either on balls hit in batting practice or by begging the ballplayers to throw an old ball up in the stands. One day Neeman was shagging balls in the outfield and I pleaded for a ball. Neeman shook his head no, turned his back to throw the ball back to the infield. But instead of sailing toward home plate, the ball flipped adroitly over his shoulder onto my lap. I'd put him on my all-time Cubbie list if I hadn't seen his throws to second base. I just can't be sure that backward flip was intentional.

There were other beauties. Clyde McCullough was the catcher of the early 50's. His swing had a hitch bigger than a Volkswagen pulling a yacht. Elvin Tappe came to the Cubs along with a publicity promotion that would have done justice to Samuel Goldwyn in his heyday. He and twin brother Melvin were going to lead the Cubs to the promised land. They didn't tell us that the promise was seventh place.

There were Dick Bertell and Randy Bobb and Tim Hosley. In case you forgot any of the 26 catchers since 1950, here is a list. If any of the averages look good to you, don't be deceived. They were attained while they played for other clubs.

CUB CATCHERS FROM 1950 TO PRESENT

Name	Career Batting Average	Year Started
Clyde McCullough	.252	1940
Rube Walker	.227	1948
Carl Sawatski	.242	1948
Smoky Burgess	.295	1949
Harry Chiti	.238	1950
Toby Atwell	.260	1952
Joe Garagiola	.257	1953
Walker Cooper	.285	1954
Jim Fanning	.170	1954
Elvin Tappe	.207	1954
Hobie Landrith	.233	1956

Name	Career Batting Average	Year Started
Charlie Silvera	.282	1957
(with Cubs	.208)	
Dale Long (2 games only)	.267	1958
Moe Thacker	.177	1958
Sammy Taylor	.245	1958
Del Rice	.237	1960
Dick Bertell	.250	1960
Jim Hegan	.228	1960
Cuno Barragan	.202	1961
Merritt Ranew	.247	1963
John Boccabella	.219	1963
Jimmy Schaffer	.223	1963
Vic Roznovsky	.218	1964
Ed Bailey	.256	1965
Chris Krug	.192	1965
Randy Hundley	.236	1966
Randy Bobb	.100	1968
Bill Plummer	.194	1968
John Felske	.135	1968
Ken Rudolph	.211	1969
Jack Hiatt	.251	1970
J. C. Martin	.222	1970
Hal Breeden	.243	1971
Chris Cannizzaro	.235	1971
Elrod Hendricks	.219	1972
Tom Lundstedt	.092	1973
George Mitterwald	.235	1974
Steve Swisher	.223	1974
Ed Putman (5 games)	.429	1976
(and he's in the minors)		
Mike Gordon	.000	1977

I was weaned on Bert Wilson. I can't remember the exact moment the Cubs became more important to me than my mother's breast. It was a meshing of the thrill of kicking a vicious shot in kindergarten kick ball games (this whetted my interest in baseball), my loathing of the White Sox, the influence of my big brother who was a Cub fan, the advertisements in the 50's urging fans to come out to beautiful Wrigley Field and have a picnic at the park (nothing was ever mentioned about the team) and the radio broadcasts of Bert Wilson.

Bert Wilson was one of the pioneers of the modern day announcer. Before him, a baseball game was described like a bar mitzvah. Players egos were not dented by disparaging remarks, spit was called saliva, and the announcer's voice was only raised if a game winning home run broke up a no-hitter in the bottom of the ninth.

Bert Wilson might have wanted to fit into this mold of the sportscaster of his day, but he couldn't. He was too "into the Cubs." The excitement overcame him so much that he finally died of a heart attack at the microphone, a testimony to his sincerity.

A home run as told by Bert Wilson sounded like its flight had defied scientific principles. What a contrast this was to the crosstown announcer, Bob Elson and his "Here we go into the 15th. 1-1 at Cleveland" (in his later years it was 1-1 at the Big A [Anaheim]). Do you realize how boring it was listening to 1-1 White Sox games at midnight west coast time?

Mr. Wilson had another super attribute. I have never heard anyone more optimistic. This guy would bet on a horse with a broken leg. How many times do I remember the Cubs trailing the Dodgers 6-1 in the ninth and Wilson saying, "If Miksis, Fondy, Baumholtz and Bolger would get on and then if Sauer would connect and hit one on Waveland Avenue, this would be a brand new ballgame." This was when I started to learn how big a word *IF* is.

I was in my pre-teens when I began hanging on every word Mr. Wilson uttered. When the Cubs were trailing (usually), Wilson would plead, "If only Handsome Ransom could connect." And of course, invariably, there would be no connection since even a good power hitter hits a home run only every 20 bats or so. The connection that Wilson cried for always seemed to me to be as monumental a technical undertaking as the Alaskan pipe line.

Being prior to the television era, we had to depend on radio descriptions to visualize what was happening. I was seven or eight and Wilson used to freak me out when he'd say, "That one is hit deep to left. Back, back, back, it's on the catwalk in left." I'd be sitting at home trying to picture a catwalk and all I could see were grinning cheshires. My imagination went wild when he started talking about the moondeck in Busch stadium, the pavilion in Ebbets Field, the light tower in Forbes Field, the incline at Crosley Field or the short left field porch in Milwaukee. And hearing about the Green Monster in Boston or the monuments in Yankee Stadium was like trying to order off a menu written in French.

Baseball parks really sounded like neat places and I thank Bert Wilson for introducing me to the game of baseball which I love and which has given me thousands of pleasurable hours.

I go through a bottle of Alka Seltzer each year on opening day. I'm always nervous the only day I'm sure the Cubs are still in the pennant fight. If anyone wants to go on a butterfly hunt, they can start right in my stomach. This is because I care. In the company of a White Sox leaner, I might feign sarcastic aloofness after a hard loss, but believe me, the pain is there. I'm up when they win, down when they lose.

After a Cub loss my brain becomes distorted. I throw my transistor radio against the wall during moments of anguish. After every tough Cubs defeat my phone will ring and my friend, Luigi, the White Sox fan, will greet me with his "hee, hee, hee, hee, hee." Then I fire the phone against the wall.

On opening day, however, all the wrist-slitting losses have long been forgotten. This will be the majestic year we have been waiting for. No other day rivals the home opener. You get presents on Christmas, a square meal on Thanksgiving, and Ground Hog's Day gives you a more reliable weather forecast than TV's professional meteorologists. That tingling, tense, anticipatory feeling that controls your whole body only comes on the day the ballclub opens the season at home.

Every fan tries to get to the ballpark. The businessmen take the afternoon off, the employees attend "their grandmother's funeral," the school kids yell, "See ya after school, ma" and then duck behind the house to head for the bus stop on the corner.

An earlier crowd than usual converges on the park this day. The most sophisticated baseball fan can feel his heart skip a beat when he gets this first glimpse of the ballpark again. You're just a block away and your pace quickens. You pass the panhandler under the elevated tracks, the souvenir stand near the tavern, the hot dog huts which live off baseball fans like parasites, through the throngs standing in front of the main gate and past the acne-faced usher into the ballpark.

The rasping voices of the vendors greet your entrance: "Scorecard, scorecard. Rrrrred hots, rrrred hots. Cold beer, beer. Cold beer, beer. Cold beer, beer." A little boy startles you when he slams the heel of his foot on an upside down beer cup a few feet away. The visiting Phillies clatter down the metal steps that lead from the clubhouse to the playing field. The spiked shoes on metal can't be heard over the insults hurled by belligerent fans. The fans watch the players as if they were gorillas behind bars in a zoo.

The players are more like zombies at first, their minds still lying on Mediterranean beaches. The pace picks up, a Santo-type snaps back at a happy heckler. The bleachers are packed, a few stragglers still climbing the concrete steps to the upper grandstand, the boxes loaded with the affluent.

"Attention, attention please." 40,000 hearts skip a beat as the ghost of Pat Pieper begins to introduce the lineup. The field is not as green as you remembered and the vines are still a scraggly brown, but it still looks better than anything you've seen in six months.

First thing the day of a game, even before a good Cub fan relieves himself, he checks the wind. He always uses the same gauge, previously selected to best determine which way the wind is blowing and at what velocity. This gauge could be the flag waving in front of the local school, the branches of the oak on the corner, or a balloon the Cub fan has saved to cut loose.

If the wind is blowing from the south out toward left field, the Cub fan can go about his day's duties without worrying once about the outcome of the ballgame. When the wind blows out at Wrigley Field, the Cubs win. The wind is to the Cubs what spinach is to Popeye.

I don't want anyone to get the impression that I just fill these pages with homespun bologna. I research, fella. For years, I have held my Cub pennant outside the window to check the wind first thing in the morning. I asked my friends if they also did it. They all said yes, that's the very first thing they do after rising. They said Cub fans have no control over this; it is a natural instinct developed during infancy in Cubbie land.

But I thought I'd better investigate further. Maybe my friends were just pulling my leg. I took a day off work to wander around Chicagoland, asking people whether they too checked to see if the wind was coming out of the south or north first thing in the morning. It was indeed true! They all did! But on days of rescheduled games, some confessed that their bodies weren't conditioned to immediately leap out of bed, and they sometimes brushed their teeth and read the sports section before being driven to the window.

Dick Orangewald, a veteran of the chemical sales rat-race, says, "I always knew my degree in chemistry would pay off. One day, when I couldn't spot an adequate wind sock, I ran into the chem lab, tossed a couple of mixtures together and came up with a dark green gas which I let out the window. I immediately noted the wind was blowing out of the southeast at 16 m.p.h."

Bob Green, a LaSalle Street barrister, reminisced about the time he failed to check the wind. "I was pleading a case in court and had no opportunity to leave. The Cub game was about to start and I still did not know which way the wind was blowing. I couldn't concentrate. At this point the Lord intervened. The judge ordered that a window be opened in the stuffy courtroom. A few minutes later he asked a witness to step into his chambers. As he walked to the door, I detected a breeze causing his robe to move from left to right. Instantly, I knew the wind was out of the south at eight m.p.h. I won the case."

Jeff Schmidt works for a large downtown bank. "I'll never figure out how it happened, but somehow I forgot to check the wind one morning. I was counting a huge pile of twenties, when suddenly I remembered. Without knowing what I was doing, I ran to the fourth floor window and started to let the bills fly. On their way down to the waiting crowds they drifted about six feet over to the left. Using a simple physics formula, I knew the wind was blowing in from the north at 21 m.p.h."

Sox fans think this wind checking business is ridiculous. Apparently up to this year they thought home runs were ridiculous. Why ruin a good day even talking about the Sox? I hope next time they go to Detroit their plane gets hijacked to Newark.

Chicago is basically a Cub town, in spite of Harry Caray. Possibly it's because of the winning years the Cubs had in the 30's, or because Wrigley Field is located on the attractive north side, or because the Cubs play all day games at home which attracts the young fans. In any event, the Cubs seem to get the best press coverage in town.

Some years back, Sox fans were tiring of hearing Bob Elson, say "Runs, hits and errors are all part of this great game of baseball," and Sox management needed to hype the sagging gate. So when Sox broadcasts were switched to WMAQ, Bob Elson was released (he now calls wrestling the greatest game in the world) and the Sox and WMAQ started looking for a new mouth who could cut into the Cubs' fandom.

About this time, Harry Caray had gotten himself fired in St. Louis after doing Cardinal games for over 20 years and after having built up hundreds of thousands of fans. This says something for Harry Caray.

Caray had been baiting the Cubs for years from St. Louis. Should the Cubs be in first place and lose and the Cardinals win, his sign off would be, "Hey Cubbies, the Cardinals are coming, tra la tra la."

The Sox decided a Cub baiter was perfect for their situation and Harry packed his six pack and moved to Chicago. All in all, things have worked out for Harry and the Sox, but the inevitable has occurred. Harry has now become bigger than the ballclub. The only thing bigger than Harry's popularity in Chicago these days is his ego. Like Howard Cosell, he is a legend in his own mind.

At one time, Harry was a very good baseball announcer. He actually told you what was happening on the field. But for the past few seasons all we've gotten is, "They're here from Glenwood, they're here from Lincolnwood, they're here from Downer's Grove (as if these suburbs within a 25 mile radius of the ballpark were not in the same hemisphere). My good friends Pete and Tom Banaka, Eli's Place for Steak, Gino and Georgetti's, Jack McHugh of the Four Torches, etc. etc. all have parties here down on restaurant row. Hey, there goes Miss Chicago. Here's Orta. He hasn't hit the ball hard in a week. Here's the pitch. He PoPPPPed it up." (Last week Harry was talking about the sweet swing Orta has and how he knew he was going to have a big year.)

I haven't seen such a frontrunner since George Romney in the 1968 Republican primaries.

And pity his fellow announcers when Harry is in a surly mood and doesn't feel like sharing the spotlight. Lorn Brown, a current sidekick, might say, "I don't think Palmer is throwing the ball like he usually does. We might get to him in the later innings. What do you say, Harry?" Harry says nothing and lets Brown's words twist quickly in the wind.

And how he loves it when they open his microphone during the home half of the seventh at Sox park and he leads the fans in a raspy rendition of "Take Me Out to the Ballgame". He is always too busy swinging his arms and basking in the moonlight (the Sox usually play night games) to catch the first note of the organist.

Harry enjoys portraying himself as the "people's man". He is as much a man of the people as Machiavelli was. Yet he has me changing channels for innings even at a time when the Cubs are playing opposite the Sox. And I listen to his games from Anaheim at midnight, west coast time. But, just give us a shot at a subway series, Harry. We'll see who goes "tra la tra la."

When I was a kid, playing ball, watching the Cubs and Sox and reading the sports pages wasn't enough. This only consumed about 12 of the 24 hours in a day and Eisenhower's speeches didn't do it for me either. What I needed was diversion from school, from taking out the garbage, from visiting Aunt Matilda in Wilmette ... in general, from life.

One rainy day in the summer, I founded the National Dice-de-Dice League. Dice-de-Dice was a game I invented using dice (hence the name), in which I could go through a major league schedule on the floor of our living room and determine my own pennant winner, my own home run champion, and my own 20 game winner.

Six-6 was a home run ... 5-5 a single ... 4-4 a single ... 3-3 a triple ... 2-2 a double ... etc. There were strike outs and sacrifice flys and double plays. Each game took 20 minutes and another ten to record the statistics. I played nine games a day (more if doubleheaders were scheduled). I could amuse myself for hours. I could do my own managing. God, how quick I was to pull pitchers who were getting slugged around by the thunderous roll of the dice. It wouldn't take me but a second to replace a weak-hitting infielder with a stronger pinchhitter regardless of whether there was a lefty or righty on the mound.

They were screwy games. My winningest pitcher was Tom Poholsky, a mediocrity in real life, and the star home run hitter was Tony Taylor, who ended up his career, 1,432nd on the all time home run leader list.

Then there was the day I had a 1-0 no-hitter going with two outs in the bottom of the ninth against Cincinnati. The average hit total in Dice-de-Dice was around 12 per team per game, so to have a no-hitter going was a mathematical improbability. I would have been on a hell of a winning (or losing) streak shooting craps in Vegas on this day. With two outs, the batter walked and the pitcher was up. I pulled him and pinchhit Gus Bell. The dice came up with boxcars ... 6-6 ... a game winning, no hit breaking home run. This was traumatic. The losing pitcher (Tom Poholsky) rolled slowly off the field. I must have stared at that 6-6 for 15 minutes. I couldn't play the rest of my schedule that day.

There were other professionally marketed kids' games in those days, but none had the appeal of Dice-de-Dice. There was the inane All Star Baseball. Every kid in America got at least one of these each birthday. How many times did I flick my finger at that little spinner, feeling if I flicked my finger harder, the player had hit the ball farther.

I remember when I sent $15.00 in to Lancaster, Pennsylvania and waited anxiously for my APBA game to arrive. The game was advertised as being 100 percent realistic. Each player in the majors would perform within a given deviation to his actual performance. For a while this replaced Dice-de-Dice, but the game took too long to play and I got turned off when the board told me one of my star players injured his wrist in an auto accident and would have to miss 25 games.

So I went back to Dice-de-Dice, ridding myself of boredom and continuing to create a problem for my parents. It was impossible to explain to guests why I lay on the floor for five solid hours, shaking dice, with a smile on my face.

The damndest thing was, the Cubs didn't even win in Dice-de-Dice.

A few diehards are still asking whether baseball is a sport or a business. It is a question that bothers baseball purists who love the sounds, sights, smell, taste and feel of the game. They let baseball fill up their senses and it is inconceivable to them that some in the baseball world are not in it just for the love of the game.

Oh, I know the ballplayers belong to a union, have agents and families to support, but I've got to believe that the thrill of putting on that major league uniform and stroking that horsehide around the field the way they did on sandlots during their youth is really what it's all about.

If the fans didn't think baseball was a sport, they wouldn't gather 40,000 strong on Sunday afternoons to cheer for their favorites. I don't recall ever seeing 40,000 people applaud a bank teller who balances out at the end of the day or a barber who cuts and styles the hair of a rambunctious five year old.

Players may spend time on income tax deductions and investments, but I know that most of them feed their souls with fadeaway slides and hitting the cut-off man.

It's true one or two of the guys follow the stock market and pick up a copy of the *Wall Street Journal* along with *Sporting News*, but I'm sure it would be all the same to them if the only market around was the one where they buy their meat.

Possibly a handful of the players won't automatically think of ballplayers when someone brings up Cash, Bonds and Money, but most of them still feel blessed that they are getting a check every two weeks for playing a little boy's game.

All you have to do is listen to the traditional chatter of baseball and there is no longer a question of whether baseball is still a game. Hanging around the dugout one day, I heard what the guys were really saying:

> "Hey, Billy, did you go with the cumulative preferred stock or the cumulative bond? I got an extrapolation of the inter-company profit and based on the insurance reserve was pleased with the scope, although I'm not happy with the scrip dividend."
>
> "I agree with you, Dusty, except you probably didn't consider the profit prior to consolidation."
>
> "Yeah, but the normal price has to be weighed against the obsolescence factor to determine whether the prospectus would be a prudent investment."
>
> "Dusty, there is something else to consider. I'll go into it with you after I bat."
>
> "Good enough. What's the score?"
>
> "Hell if I know."

I cried long and hard when Jack Quinlan, my favorite Cub announcer and one of the best baseball announcers of all time, was tragically killed in a semi-tractor trailer accident in Arizona during spring training in 1965.

I had lost a special friend. I couldn't count the times I smuggled a transistor with an earphone into study hall in high school or left the premises at work during summer jobs to catch a portion of the broadcast. My family was stationed in Germany in the early 60's, and I would hear his rich, clear voice over the Armed Forces Network across the Atlantic (it was always the Cubs because they played in the afternoon, which was evening in Europe).

Hearing him talk about "the friendly confines of beeyootifull Wrigley Field" when I was 3000 miles away was like hearing the rescue team when you are trapped in a coal mine cave-in.

Quinlan was a humorous Vin Scully, a Cub enthusiast who could make you believe their 65-80 record here in September showed signs of promise and it wasn't foolhardy to pull for Moose Moryn to get a hit in the next to last game of the season.

Lou Boudreau, the Hall of Famer and a member of the present Cub broadcast team, teamed up with Quinlan as the color man in the early 60's. Boudreau was no Hall of Famer in the booth. By the time he finished describing a play, you were getting your car out of the parking lot. He was as articulate as J. Fred Muggs. But Quinlan saw the diamond in the rough and worked closely with Lou developing an announcing style and bringing out Boudreau's baseball expertise. They gave us comic relief when we needed it badly. The high point of one broadcasting season came when it took Lou half an inning to read a panty hose commercial because Quinlan couldn't stop laughing.

I'm sorry Jack Quinlan never got to broadcast Cub games when their teams had any semblance of respectability. During Quinlan's years, the light at the end of the tunnel was fifth place.

Two weeks after a spaceflight is forced to scrap its mission, NASA is able to explain the failure. It has only taken me five days to analyze the reason for the stoppage of the Cubs winning skeins so far this year. The Cub ballplayers have been changing their underwear.

There are some ancient maxims in baseball which must be followed if you expect to win ballgames. Never, they say, put the winning run on base, never walk the opposing pitcher, and never change your underwear during a winning streak. I have discovered that after wearing the same set of underwear for six straight games, many of the ballplayers have insisted that they be allowed to change their undergarments. I've heard that Manager Franks threatened to fine any player who switched underwear, even if they switched to a pair of the colored underwear his predecessor, Durocher, had been promoting on TV.

Still, I know of at least three players who did change their underwear. I refuse to name names here, but they are the same players who never get their uniforms dirty during the games.

If Franks were not only a superstitious sort, but also suspicious, he would have known why the Cubs stopped winning. It wasn't because of poor hitting and pitching. The culprit was clean underwear. If Franks was an industrious manager who really cared, he would have held an underwear check before each game.

In all fairness, there might have been contributing factors to the Cubs recent losses. Steve Ontiveras might have forgotten to touch third base after the third out of an inning, Manager Franks might have accidentally stepped on the chalk line on one of his trips to the mound, General Manager Kennedy might have forgotten to wear his daffodil, or one of the players might have taken a different route to the park than normal.

Whatever it was, it has to stop. I'm positive that if every person connected with the Cubs would carefully carry out their superstitions to the smallest detail, the Cubs would almost for sure go undefeated. I mean what does pitching, hitting and fielding have to do with baseball anyway?

In May, I loaded my typewriter in the car and followed the Cubs to Cincy.

I had made reservations in the Netherland Hilton in Cincinnati (the same establishment which houses the Cubs) through the Hilton out-of-town reservation office in Chicago. Much to my chagrin when I arrived in the City of Seven Hills (as Cincinnati is called, I'm told), the friendly Netherland Hilton people informed me they had no record of my reservation and the hotel was filled. I could believe the hotel was filled alright. There must have been 1500 Bleacher Bums from Chicago strolling around the lobby, guzzling beer, walking around in their undershirts and responding to their bugler's urgings by intermittently yelling "charge" at the top of their lungs.

Meanwhile, I was still standing in the lobby roomless and fearing that I might at any moment be picked up on vagrancy charges. I went back to the desk and demanded that the room clerk re-check for record of my reservation. He went away and two seconds later came back claiming he had searched all over without success. I then demanded that he check with the Chicago Hilton office. He assured me that the office in Chicago would be closed. I couldn't understand why the Chicago office would be closed at 4:00 in the afternoon, so I placed an indignant collect call to Chicago. The Hilton people there, a little more sophisticated than the Cincinnati group, instructed me to ask for the assistant manager in five minutes. In the interim they would wire the assistant manager and ask him to find accommodations for me. Five minutes later, I was given the key to Room 2824. Herman Franks was staying in Room 2822.

Cincinnati's new ballpark, Riverfront Stadium, has one major fault. They built it on the riverfront. This means there is limited access to and from the ballpark, since you can't get to the park by way of the river unless you're a porpoise. The other side of the park adjoins a series of expressways. The people who designed the area cleverly placed two overpasses leading from the stadium across the expressway. It must have looked great on their drawing boards. Practically speaking, however, as soon as the game ends, there are 50,000 people trying to cross two overpasses. The first night I was at the game, it took exactly one hour for us to get across the expressway. Other than this, the park is fine ... except for the fact you see vendors as often as you see porpoises in the Ohio River ... except for the fact there are about ten ushers in the entire stadium ... except for the fact that many areas of the park smell like vomit ... except for the fact the drinking fountains don't work ... except for the fact that the Reds were World Champions in 1975 and 1976.

They should build new stadiums old. The new parks lack the charisma of the old stadiums. My pet peeve is the mechanical cheerleading used in all the new parks to generate enthusiasm. True fans don't have to be told when to cheer.

Sometimes, when the Cubs are bad, I have to get away from it all. I try sleep, but closing my eyes all I see are topped grounders, towering pop-ups and lunging swings.

Last Saturday, instead of heading for Wrigley Field, I went to the Waveland Public Golf Course with my trusty radio (held together by bandages following a recent Cub fiasco) and Stosh.

I had a great day planned, except I should have realized the only thing worse than seeing the Cubs play and lose a 17 inning game is attempting to play golf at a public course on a Saturday afternoon. It's not simply the tremendous wait you must endure before teeing off to begin the round and between every subsequent shot as much as the inane golf comments you're forced to listen to while waiting.

A twosome never has a chance to get off at a public course. The starter will always match you up with another twosome or two singles who can't find anyone who wants to play golf with them. But brother, they found you.

You'll be standing to the side practicing your swing when the loudspeaker blares out "12:38 on the tee. Come on fellas. 12:38." As you head for the tee you note the starter has stuck to the public course schedule. It's now 2:08 and he's exactly one and one half hours behind. About this time some schlemiel will approach and ask if you mind if he plays along. Lying, you say no. Another one pops up: "Hi, I'm Bobby Golfball." The foursome is complete and you're ready to start.

I'm first, and after going through my patented mannerisms while addressing the ball, I'm ready to hit. As I bring the clubhead back in the backswing, the loudspeaker blares out, "Okay fellas. Tee off. Hit away. 12:44 is next." The ball goes shooting off to the right.

I'm about to break the driver over my knee when the schlemiel says, "That'll play. It won't kill you. You're out there okay. That one might bring rain."

Bobby Golfball is nodding, "Good stroke. You got a nice roll. You'll be able to hook it around the tree alright."

Ten minutes later you line your second shot off a tree into the lake. You fling your club 20 yards up the fairway. You're sweating and cussing.

I had a fantastic round. I started the day with ten clubs and came back in with the same ten. Besides that, I had a hole in one. The other sock was okay, though.

Let me tell you about my round. On the first hole, I popped a short one up the middle, I topped my three wood, hooked a five iron, overshot the green with a nine iron, chipped on and two putted for an opening seven.

On the second hole, I hit a ground ball to the left, smashed a three wood 30 yards from the green, chipped on and two putted for a bogey five.

On the third hole ... wait a second. Even I'm bored with this. People talking about their golf games are as bad as having them show you films of their last vacation.

Nothing went right that day. I got a parking ticket, broke my sun glasses, and the banana milkshake I had for lunch was rancid. Next time I'll take my chances at the ballpark.

Prior to the opening of the baseball season, I always send letters and resumes to all the major league baseball teams indicating my desire to become associated with their organization in some capacity and explaining what my qualifications are.

Every year I say, "Gentlemen: Still hopeful, still enthusiastic, and more importantly, still qualified." Every year they say, "Thank you for your letter. We are impressed with your qualifications. However, baseball openings do not occur with great frequency and nothing is available at this time. We will keep your application on file and should anything come up, we will keep you in mind."

I know it is tough to land a job in baseball, and I could have accepted the answers the baseball people have given me until David Eisenhower's appointment a few years ago to a position with the Washington Senators. David was hired to accumulate statistics from the minor league games for the minor league players in the Washington Senator system.

I can't understand why Eisenhower got the job. I used to apply for a job with the Senators regularly, and each time they assured me that no openings were available. Surely my credentials were equal to Eisenhower's. My knowledge of the game surpasses his. My journalism degree would seem more appropriate than his history degree. I'd be able to travel often and extensively. I could work immediately and continually throughout the year without having to take time out to visit the Japanese exposition a few weeks after I accepted the job. I don't understand it. Maybe he knew someone.

I've always felt that Walter Jacobson, of Channel Two news, had the same yearnings as I. The closest he came to being a professional athlete was as a batboy for the Cubs.

It's not that reading the news is so dull. The shuffling of all those papers does, however, become laborsome for one as small as Walter.

Walter is obviously a frustrated athlete. His size has always been a hindrance. Even now, it has created a problem for Channel Two, who have hired leading architects to design a chair high enough to allow their cameras to get Bill Kurtis and Walter in the same picture.

Jacobson was a bright kid. After failing to budge anyone in gym class football games (including the kid with asthma) and after being unable to get a shot off in the basketball games, he quickly eliminated pursuing a career in these sports. On a whim, he did go to a Bear tryout camp, but when he saw they had a 250 pound water-boy, he pointed his tricycle back towards Chicago. He came to the conclusion that he was only suited to be a jockey but, at the time, there were more jockeys than horses.

Then, the same nepotism, cronyism or other ism's that he heatedly decrys on his Perspective segment worked for him. He got a job as the Chicago Cub batboy. Walter knew someone. There are one-half million kids in Chicago who would love this job each summer, but all their connections will get them is a job picking up paper for the park district.

Oh, how Walter loved his job. He would jump joyfully to the friendly snarls, "Hey, kid, shine my spikes." Handing the towels to these mediocre physical specimens (afterall, these were the Cubs) as they advanced to the shower is a job beyond description. The job was also a learning process. Picking up the dirty underwear from the locker room floor was Walter's start in investigative reporting. It was over too soon. At 23, when Walter began to shave, he was released by the Cubs. Walter bummed around for years drifting from one station to another when WBBM took a chance on the aging leprauchan.

Walter has done well at Channel Two. Aldermen around town shake like weeping willow trees in a tornado when they run into Jacobson. But there's one story he's never told. Give us the inside dope some night, Walter. How *did* you become the Cub's batboy?

When he screams the players jump. On days he is in a foul mood, they stay clear of him. He wields power. He'll never tell them to hit behind the runner, but he does make big decisions. He has been with the club since I was a child. Yosh Kawano, the clubhouse man, may be the reason the Cubs have gotten no respect in the past 32 years.

Mr. Kawano is Japanese. Perhaps I have seen too many World War II movies in which Japanese were the enemy. I have this image of Kawano calling up the Pirates after everyone has left the clubhouse saying, "Allo, this is Kawano. When Franks scratch stomach, that mean double steal. When pick nose, that mean squeeze play. When scratch ass, that mean itch."

Until the Cubs document these calls, Kawano runs the clubhouse with a karate chop. If he likes you, life is but a dream. Your locker is near the shower and the uniform fits. Should a ballplayer misjudge his power and slight him, bad things simultaneously happen. The locker assigned is between the pizza and peanut vendors. The spikes given have three cleats on one foot and five on the other. The uniform number he gives out has a degrading connotation such as 32 1/8. Phone calls are forwarded to the Wichita Aeros clubhouse. When the player asks for something to nibble on he is given a bat.

Yosh Kawano has been with the Cubs long enough to see the greats come and go (not first place greats — fifth place greats). Despite being the clubhouse man, a traditional messenger boy position, Kawano has been no flunky. The players know he's got the gloves, got the bats and got the balls.

Vince Lloyd became the radio voice of the Cubs, joining Lou Boudreau after Jack Quinlan's death. Prior to this, Lloyd lived in virtual anonymity as Jack Brickhouse's sidekick on the telecasts. There wasn't wholesale jubilation when Lloyd was given the radio assignment. He had been with WGN for years without building a following. His voice was not sun kissed. It was and is more like a thunderstorm.

But Vince has a place in the hearts of Cub fans. Vince is also a fan. He's not simply selling the team. Just tune in the post-game wrap-up and listen to the inflection in his voice. If you missed the game, you don't have to wait for a score to see if the Cubs won or lost. There is a certain ardor in his voice when he has a winner to re-cap. When the Cubs lose, his vocal cords go limp.

Vince and Lou have become as familiar a pair as Abbott and Costello, or Donny and Marie. Imagine inviting someone into your home 162 times a year for over ten years. They'd either have to be the postman or your brother-in-law.

Like Costello, sometimes Vince doesn't know who's on first. But Boudreau knows who it is, why he got there, and when he might decide to mosey on down to the next base. Lou knows baseball, Vince knows broadcasting and they mesh their respective talents admirably.

One gift they share is their ability to devour huge quantities of food before, during and after the game. What beer is to Harry, corned beef on rye is to Vince and Lou. The listeners are always given a running total on who has consumed what and when the diets will begin (always the next day). The food talk is like a vicious circle. Since Boudreau and Lloyd obviously appreciate a tasty snack, little old ladies from Hoopeston, Illinois bring the ravished announcers homemade egg salad on their annual trip to Wrigley Field.

Cub fans are patient people, as our 32 losing years without a revolution will ascertain, so when Vince and Lou get too excited to explain what's going on, we uncomplainingly wait for Vince's two or three holy mackerels and for Lou's breath to catch up with him before finding out how the play went.

What endears this dynamic duo most to Cub fans is their down-to-earth sincerity and friendliness. When I was in college, I visited the Cubs spring training base in Arizona during spring break. Before one of their exhibition games, I saw Vince and Lou in the nearby pressbox and introduced myself to them. I was taken aback at the firm handshakes and straight-in-the-eye looks they gave me as I explained how they could improve their broadcasting style.

Despite what Wally Phillips says, these two men are grand slam bellringers.

Speaking of Wally Phillips, many Cub fans listen to his program religiously every morning for the sports segment between 8:15 and 8:30. Highlights of the previous day's ballgame are replayed and *Tribune* columnist, Rick Talley, will chit-chat with Wally just for the sake of chit-chat. The best thing about this quarter hour is that there is actually more discussion than commercials.

My clock radio comes on early every morning to the reassuring tone of WGN and Chicago's number one morning man. It's a routine I and millions of mid-westerners adhere to every morning, but I can't explain why. I don't really need to know how many cattle are taken to the Peoria markets each day. Nor do I need to know the price of soybean futures.

Then there are the endless inane calls.

"Wally, I can't believe I got through. I've been holding on since Tuesday."

"Well, thank you for being so patient."

I lapse back into sleep and am awakened by the next call.

"Good morning. What can I do for you?"

"I want to speak to Wally."

"This is Wally."

"You sound so different."

(Wally never seems to get upset over this. He gets upset at nothing short of child pornographers. He is the perennial good guy. Sometimes he goes too far.)

"No, this is really me."

"Well, Wally, I just want to say I'm really proud of the Cubs."

"Yes, the whole city is. And let's not forget the White Sox."

This wakes me up. I, like every true Cub fan, hope the Sox arrive in Kansas City and find out they forgot to pack their jock straps.

The next caller wants to know whether Wally has a quiz going. Wally says he'll find a question and asks, "Who was buried in Grant's tomb?" The caller doesn't know, but Wally gives him a free dinner at Mel Markon's anyway. The next caller just wants to know if he can have a free dinner. Wally figures why not, this guy has probably been hanging on since Monday, sends him to Mama Luigi's and then cuts away to Sgt. Ed and his traffic report.

"The Edens is jammed from Lake to the junction. The Kennedy Expressway is a parking lot from the junction to downtown. Estimated travel time is two hours. An alternate suggestion. Try any side street, it should cut traveling time in half. And now over to Jim Cavenaugh in traffic copter number two."

"And the Dan Ryan is bumper to bumper from 95th to 47th, it's clear sailing from 47th to 45th and it's a mass of steel from 45th on in. Remember, the steering wheel is there for your use. Use it. Now back to the WGN studios."

Back to a William A. Lewis commercial, General Finance spot, First National Bank spiel, another call, three more advertisements, more traffic updates, the stock market report, the 9:30

news, some chatter, banter, prattle and gossip and Wally Phillips calls it a day, still in first place with an insurmountable lead.

Nothing depresses me more than watching the Cubs complete nine laborsome innings of sickly fly balls and feeble rollers that accumulate one or two runs. I would rather see the White Sox win a ballgame (if it's meaningless enough) than watch the Cubs slump at the plate.

When the Cubs hitting is in low gear, they should employ a hitting theory I have advocated for years. Rogers Hornsby used to agree with me on this, but since he's passed away, I am the sole surviving supporter of this slump-breaking maneuver. In baseball circles, it's known as the Schwab/Hornsby Theory.

If I was running a waning ballclub, I would *order* my hitters to concentrate exclusively on hitting the ball up the middle. Forget about pulling the ball down the lines or hitting behind the runner. Just try to ricochet liners off the pitcher's shin bone, forehead or whatever. Even when someone is not in a slump, this is a good practice to get into. Many a base hit has fallen in the fertile area between the pitcher's mound and the center fielder. If you can get the ball past the pitcher who is generally off balance and only 60 feet away, chances are you're on base.

By concentrating entirely on hitting the ball directly up the middle, the hitter may correct the flaws which originally caused him to slump.

In an attempt to place his hit up the middle and not just any where in the ballpark, he is forced to keep his eye riveted on the ball. In doing this he will keep his head down and his shoulders straight. His swing will be smoother and the batter will not be as likely to overswing since he is not trying to pull the ball. After he gets a few hits, the confidence will return, and he might go on a hot streak.

Even if it doesn't work at the ballpark, the Schwab/Hornsby Theory ought to improve his golf score.

It was pouring that morning in 1970 when I woke up thinking about Ernie Banks. There was no chance for him to hit his 500th today. The storm put the lights out at my office for about an hour at ten a.m. Miraculously, it cleared up by noon and the game started on time.

I knew this game was going to be unique when the Braves scored two runs on a wild pitch in the first inning. If Banks wasn't going for 500 that day, I would have switched channels. "Edge of Night" had as much appeal. But, this was the day Ernie Banks hit his 500th homer. There was nothing prodigious about the home run, in fact it never rose higher than the second row of bleacher seats, but it meant more to me as a Cub fan than anything else they had ever achieved. For you see, I have been a Banks fan more than a Cub fan for all these years.

I have seen thousands of players come and go. None of them have affected my life and given me the vicarious thrills as has Ernie Banks.

When he stepped to the plate in a crucial situation, I felt for him like he was my own flesh and blood. I reveled in his glory and cringed in times of defeat. And hundreds, no thousands, of times pure emotion has come gushing forth when he overcame the odds in super-heroic fashion.

I grew up with Ernie Banks. When he first joined the Cubs, I was seven years old and just starting to love the game of baseball. At first I was attracted to his fantastic ability. Playing with the lightly regarded Cubs, here was a man the opposition actually feared.

As I watched and got to know Ernie's personality and character, I loved him as a human being. The cheerfulness, optimism, determination, diplomacy, sportsmanship and appreciation he exemplifies are the traits every father would like to instill in his son.

Ernie Banks is the human spirit participating in a sport which severely tests the complete individual. Ability, teamwork, temperment, desire and the power to bounce back from defeat are needed. Mr. Cub gets superior ratings in each of these areas. That is why he is among the most loved players in baseball history.

The love that was generated at Wrigley Field when Ernie hit one is a memory to cherish. The ovations that greeted Ernie's home runs came from the heart. I wish Ernie were in the line-up today.

By 9:30 in the morning, two lines have formed, stretching one block down Waveland and Sheffield. The people willing to wait one and a half hours until the gates open must have stamina and devotion.

The fans are predominantly under 20. Rowdy teenage boys louder than Christmas trees and threesomes of cigarette-puffing teenage girls in halter tops and cuf-off jeans. The clothes they wear make them look halfway decent ... halfway.

Around 10:30, the men "between permanent jobs" arrive with their rickety souvenir stands, hoping to hustle a livelihood. A young boy immediately purchases a Cub hat, bringing a shortlived smile to the vendor's face. A Good Humor truck pulls up, taking customers away from a graying man selling equally good ice cream from a pushcart.

Time drags and the trivia games begin. "Who was the Cubs' third baseman in the late fifties?"

"What's his initials? Never mind, Johnny Goryl."

It's a few minutes to 11, and the line tightens. At 11:00, it inches tormentingly toward the bleacher ticket booth, past the elderly ticket-taker up to the ramp leading to the uncomfortable green benches in the sun.

The bleachers are as important to the Cubs as a solid, line drive hitter. It is here, hours before the game, that the fan-player rapport is nurtured.

A ten-year old yells, "Jerry, JERREE" at Morales, who is concentrating on limbering up and winks at the greeting. The Cubs go through their well-organized pre-game practice. Balls are hit in every direction, but no one gets struck by the flying missiles.

The visiting Atlanta Braves go through their fielding practice, and the hecklers come out of the woodwork. "Hey, Burroughs, why don't you leave here and go to the zoo? You'll be less conspicuous there." "I hear they named a cake for you — a crumb cake."

The remnants of the 1969 Bleacher Bums are also still there, not as clever as the true hecklers, but just as enthusiastic. "Hey, Burroughs, ya tink you're a big cheese. Ya only smell like one."

A Bum told me once why they keep coming to games. "Dem Cubbies need us's encouragement. We encrunge them to dos good. The gooder dey duz, the betters we feels. Also, the more beers we drinks, the betters we feels."

Actually, the term Bleacher Bums is a cruel description of the people sitting out there. They're not really bums. They're just a bunch of college and high school kids who have cut classes or decided not to get a summer job. They're adult men who don't have the temperament, ability or desire to work for a living. They're people who realize for $1.50 they can stay in Wrigley Field for seven hours without being harassed by the police. They're not bums, they're just hobos, tramps or riff-raff.

The game begins and, by the second inning, the sun's rays become oppressive. A light breeze and the beer vendor are the only antidote.

The Cubs fall behind and the pre-game buoyancy dissipates. Those who aren't sunstruck or drunk desperately want the Cubs to win. That is, after all, what they're really there for.

Gamblers Anonymous should recruit in the Cubs bleachers. When the Sun God makes an appearance at Wrigley Field during a Cub home stand, the bleachers are filled beyond fire regulation capacity.

The Bleacher Bums, that egocentric collection of sun worshippers, drunks, fanatical Cub fans and kids, also includes the cast from Guys and Dolls. In Guys and Dolls, the characters included Harry The Horse, Sky Masterson, Nathan Detroit and Nicely-Nicely. In the Wrigley Field bleachers, they all sit in their customary spots, dollar bills in hand, and nervously await the next pitch. That next pitch always has more bets riding on it than Seattle Slew had at the Derby.

Handicapping a pitch is infinitely more difficult than handicapping some nag at Sportsmans Park. Sky Masterson was supposedly willing to wager on which of two raindrops would reach the bottom of the window pane first, a bet, I suggest, that is much easier to make than which pitch will be fouled off into the screen behind the plate, or in what inning the umpire will toss out the first dirty ball.

Most of the fans in the grandstands are truly dedicated to the Cubs, and they live and die by the next pitch in terms of its relationship to the ultimate outcome of the game. The degenerate Harry The Horses, however, couldn't care less whether or not the Cubs win or lose (unless they have 7-5 on the result). This distresses me. I am not opposed to gambling, but I am strongly against allowing these loyaless plungers to occupy a seat that a sufferer of 32 years better deserves. These Cub games are, after all, the substance of life, and the bookmakers would be just as satisfied betting on whether or not Idi Amin has syphilis.

One day I approached Ray, of Rays Bleachers, about the possibility of establishing an off park betting facility in his mustard emporium, to rid us of these creeps. Between chews on his rubbery Vienna, Ray seemed interested as long as he could also have the rights to off park messenger services for the entire Chicagoland area. The next day, however, the Illinois Legislature banned off track messenger services, and Ray said he was afraid the same honor would be accorded his off park service.

That afternoon, when I entered the park two hours before game time, Harry the Horse was busily handicapping which inning a ball would get stuck in the left center field vines.

There has been a vacuum in Chicago radio talk programming since Leo's Lip departed the airwaves. Whitey Lockman and Jim Marshall, the managers who followed Durocher, were as exciting as career civil service workers closing in on their pensions. Herman Franks, the current manager, has too much money to be concerned with picking up another hundred on a daily sports program. He's concentrating on buying up the state of Utah and developing it into a giant shopping center.

Some of the finest moments in life for the overwrought, neurotic Cub fans used to come around the wireless in the evening when they listened to 90 soothing minutes from Leo during which he explained why the fans should not worry about the three errors committed in clutch situations or the fact that four relief pitchers all failed miserably.

Leo, along with the wishy-washy moderator Bill Berg (maybe yes - maybe no), parried the most challenging, thoroughly researched questions hurled at them by the baseball public. Without blinking an eye or losing his last hair, Leo once spoke out on the brain-teasing controversy of the day: "Who was the best ballplayer you ever saw?" Leo answered, "Willie Mays, and I saw a lot of him, fella. He was on my ballclub with the Giants in the fifties you know. He's some kind of player. Why, he'd go out there and do it all for you. Run, throw, hit, field, everything. He'd give you 125 percent. He had desire and determination. And he's some kind of boy off the field too, I want to tell ya. He's the greatest player I ever had." The next question from the caller was, "Who's the greatest player you ever managed?"

The moderator would press another button and in his saccharine, syrupy tone says, "You're on the air with Leo. Go ahead, please."

Leo, sounding like a lion with a toothache says, "Hello o o o."

The caller says, "Hello, Leo?"

Leo says, "Hello .... Hello."

The caller says, "Leo?"

Leo says, "Yes, go ahead."

The caller says, "Okay........Leo? Are you there?"

Leo, "Yes. Yes. Go ahead."

Moderator interrupting, "Turn down your radio, please."

The caller in the distance yelling viciously to his wife, "Turn off the damn radio."

Leo to Bill Berg, "I can't hear him, Bill. We better move on to another call."

Bill Berg, "Okay, Leo."

The caller just a second before Bill Berg presses the button, "Hello, Leo? Leo, are you there?"

And then another call.

Bill Berg to the next caller, "You're on the air with Leo. Go ahead, please."

The caller, "Hello, Leo. My name is Charley Schwartz from the north side of Chicago."

Leo, "Yes, Billy."

The caller, "I have a new defensive shift I think the Cubs should use. When the Cubs get two strikes on a tough hitter like Willie McCovey, I think they should remove the catcher and play him in the outfield. That way you'll have four outfielders and a better chance of catching his line drive."

Leo, "That's an idea, Ralphie, I'll think about it."

And yet another call.

Caller, "Leo, why did you play Hundley every inning of every exhibition and regular season game last year and then advise him to play winter ball in the Caribbean League? You know he gets tired during the season. Why don't you rest him?"

Leo, "Yes, I know fella. But he loves to play and I can't get the uniform off his back with a razor blade."

Caller, "Why don't you simply tell him that he's not playing today?"

Leo, "He hates to sit out a game. He just won't do it."

Caller, "Who's the manager, Leo, you or him?"

Leo, "Now you're getting me riled, fella. Where's your manners? Everyone knows the Cubs were mired in the bottom of the league until I got here and now we have one of the most exciting teams in baseball. We came in second last year, fella, and we should have finished first if my guys hadn't played like girls the last month of the season. And I'll tell you something, fella, we're going to end up first this season. All I got to do is find some way of keeping my regulars like Hundley strong in September."

Time runs out. Once again the show acted as a tonic for the troubled Cub fan. He had renewed faith in his ballclub and quashed the anxieties that were building inside.

As for Leo, there was happiness in knowing his show was a service to baseball fans. There was security in knowing he won 95 percent of the arguments concerning his baseball strategy, even if half of the callers were 12 year olds. And there was ecstasy in thinking of the vast amount of money he got for appearing on the program.

Cubs players can't take the heat. Playing half the schedule under the sun at Wrigley Field drains their energy. All other things being equal, the Cubs must have better pitching strength and bench depth than the other contenders to win a pennant. The heat is a factor every year, but becomes far more noticeable when the Cubs are in a pennant race. In years when the Cubs are only in a race to finish the game and go home, the hot sun of July and August makes them appear woozier than they are. But in these woozy years, it is hard to tell just what is making them woozy.

The fatigue factor caused by playing day after day under the sun packs a lethal punch. The sun's energy, like a money-hungry millionaire, thrives on sapping desire from the vulnerable athletes trying to earn a livelihood under its domain. A relief pitcher trudges more slowly to the mound, a hitter's bat becomes heavier, the shimmering distance between the bases stretches into infinity; in short, the hot sun baking the ballpark causes problems for everyone but the ice cream vendor.

The last time the Cubs had a sizeable lead late in the year was in 1969. Then the sun addled Durocher's brain and he insisted on playing Santo, Beckert, Kessinger, Hundley, Williams and Hickman every day in 90° temperatures. The lead melted. Randy Hundley went from 195 pounds at the start of that season to 168 at the end, and he wasn't on the Last Chance Diet.

The effect of the sun's rays is an intangible factor which sportwriters can't measure when they make their predictions at the start of the year. But there are ways to combat it.

1) The Cubs could play their home games at seven in the morning (but what a downer to see Jack Brickhouse right after you wake up).

2) Play the games at seven in the evening and wear glow in the dark uniforms. (Didn't Bill Veeck try that once?)

3) Borrow the White Sox short shorts uniforms and wear sandals instead of spikes.

4) Adopt Claes Oldenberg's suggestion of constructing a 30-storey fan in Lake Michigan to direct the cooling breezes to Wrigley Field.

5) Replace the foul pole with the North Pole.

There might be other reasons why the Cubs haven't won in 32 years. Cub fans love their Wrigley Field and their day baseball, but since 1945 when night baseball became the staple of other teams' home schedules, the Cubs have not won a pennant. When the weather gets hot in Chicago, the Cubs get cold.

It's time labor started negotiating baseball into the workingman's contracts. The most sadistic torture ever designed is perpetrated on the baseball fan by his employer on game days. Although many teams play primarily at night on weekdays, and Mondays are traditionally off days for major league teams, it is inevitable that weekday afternoon games coincide with work. At these times, the bosses of the world exert all their power to outmaneuver their underlings as they plot ways to sneak away for a quick glimpse of a tavern's colored TV.

Highly disciplined fans try to control their emotions and casual conversation well enough so as to disguise being baseball freaks. Realistically speaking though, it never works. Large companies, I'm told, hire undercover men to mingle among the workers and seek out those likely to be distracted from their work during the baseball season. Luckily, it is easy to spot these baseballcos (the derogatory term for the undercover men). They are the strangers who one day sit at your table during the coffee break and without warning say: "The Cubs won a close one yesterday." The experienced baseball freak who has been persecuted in the past merely stares straight ahead, controlling his cheek muscles from issuing a tell-tale twitch. The more emotional baseball freak might grunt assent to the stranger's statement. The naive baseball freak says, "That's for sure. Bonham was losing his stuff in those middle innings but reached back for that something extra when he needed it." The baseballco grins and moves on to another table.

There are some brash baseball freaks who don't seem to care who knows that they are avid fans. At their job interviews, many of my friends tip their hands right away by inquiring about the company's rules concerning bringing portable Sony TV sets to work and whether opening day is a paid holiday.

My friend, Luigi, the White Sox fan, has lost two jobs in the last year because of his perverse excesses. Last summer he was working for a paint factory and was sent packing when the plant foreman caught him hiding in a paint barrel with his transistor.

And just the other day, he was given his outright release by an insurance company for his shenanigans. The White Sox were involved in a one run ballgame and Luigi didn't dare leave his desk. Thinking quickly, Luigi phoned his wife, who switched on her radio and left it blaring away while she went about her housework. Luigi was listening contentedly when he was asked to deliver a stack of insurance policies to another department. He put the White Sox game on hold and left. Luigi's department head, needing to make an urgent call to San Francisco, grabbed one of Luigi's extension phones and was flabbergasted to hear Harry Caray's beer-soaked voice saying, "Ground ball to short. Bannister's up with it, over to first. Out."

He started to push the button up and down in an unsuccessful attempt to get a dial tone, hearing intermittently such inanities as, "Oscar Gamble stepping to the plate. Sox are down by a run. C'mon Oscar, punch one."

When Luigi returned to his desk some 15 minutes later (he had snuck downstairs to watch the sixth inning in a bar), he was asked to leave, *AT ONCE!* He has a lot of time to spend at Sox games these days. Serves him right!

In recent years, if nothing else, we've had clean livers for managers. Whitey Lockman, Jim Marshall and Herman Franks are all men you'd bring home for dinner (except with Herman you'd lock the refrigerator door). The shame that Leo Durocher brought to the club during his rampages still sticks in Cub fans' craws.

I remember an incident in a Cub-Atlanta game when Manager Durocher was fined and suspended for making obscene gestures. Most Cub fans did not realize Durocher was capable of such crude behavior. We felt Leo was a genial, elderly man who enjoyed sitting in the sun during the summer months making helpful suggestions to the more inexperienced players.

I was watching WGN-TV when its camera crew focused on Leo making those signals toward Umpire Tony Venzon. I kept telling myself that Leo, a knight in shining armor to the youth of this country, would not, could not, conduct himself in such a manner. My faith in what is good would be shattered if a man of Leo's stature employed such street corner habits.

Some of the older baseball fans I know gently informed me that indeed Mr. Durocher might have used his middle finger to show disrespect. Then I learned Mr. Durocher did not always attend religious services each Sunday. Next I discovered that Leo's nickname "The Lip" was not given to him because of public speaking prowess but because of his obnoxious baiting of fellow ballplayers and umpires. On top of this, Durocher was a divorced man. I was crushed.

Things started to fall in place. I remembered the Schlitz commercial when Leo was telling how he liked to kick the lye on the umpire's suit. There was a gleam in his eye when he noted that the lye would burn a hole in the umpire's pants' leg.

I also remember years back when Leo first took over the Cubs. He called Ernie Banks "Old Grandpa" and talked of replacing him with a younger player. He discarded this plan only after word reached him that the fans planned to hang him by his ankles from the center field scoreboard.

In spring trainings past, Durocher lied brazenly. He talked about Don Young being his center fielder when everyone knew Young had as much chance to stay with the Cubs as Agnew had to become a professional golfer. When Durocher disliked someone, he was gone. Durocher talked of the help he would get in center field from Jimmy Qualls, Al Spangler and Jimmy McMath. He told the Cub fans that the Cubs would be stronger because of Roe Skidmore, Jim Cosman, Randy Bobb, Roger Metzger, Dave Lemonds, Darcy Fast and other nobodys. Rumor has it that the Soviets have asked Durocher to head their propaganda program.

I learned to live with your imperfections, Leo. But not on TV. Not in front of the kiddies. Say your gestures weren't obscene. Say it ain't so, Leo. Say you were merely swatting a swarm of gnats from in front of your face when you were making that funny motion with your hand.

The toughest Cub fan wets his pants at the thought of a subway series.

For the first time in 72 years, the possibility exists of a city series between the Cubs and the White Sox. The few times two clubs from the same city have made it to the World Series, the October classic has been known as a subway series, since both ballparks could be reached by public transportation.

Cub fans can easily come to grips with playing the White Sox, and don't even fear losing to them since there are far more Cub fans and we would slaughter them should they become too obnoxious.

What we do fear is riding the subways to get to the ballparks. Our local transportation network, the CTA (Catastrophies Twice Annually), has a safety record equivalent to that of the Three Stooges. They have accidents that cause traffic jams for hours, and I'm only talking about the ones in their yards.

What is even more frightening than their motormen is their clientele.

I remember once heading for Wrigley Field as a youth on the Jackson Park el, which passes through miles of black ghetto. Me, a white kid, traveling a stagecoach through Indian country.

This one day, the el stopped and Cochise and his tribe boarded the train and proceeded to scalp me and my friends out of a Ted Lepcio model glove, $10.00, a watch and four brown bags containing assorted bologna and peanut butter sandwiches.

For a brief moment I thought we would thwart the robbery in progress when a big husky man showed up. I asked him to get the other fellows to leave us alone. "Give 'em a few dimes and quarters, kid" he hollered as he took off for the next car.

I have never seen a security man ride the el, or, in fact, anyone who looks mentally competent.

The only thing that makes me feel good about the Chicago Transit Authority is that their record through the years has been just as poor as the Cubs, although they've come up with a few more upsets.

The Cubs' management

has panicked only once in the post-war years despite the club's horrendous record. This was in 1961 when they employed 11 managers in one season. This is easily a major league record (although the Texas Rangers are challenging it this year). If you want to get technical, the Cubs had 11 coaches and no manager since they were all created equal by P. K. Wrigley, who innovated the idea. The theory was young Cub players would benefit from the tutelage of the 11 wise men who could impart their special area of expertise. In addition, the Cub coaches would rotate through the farm system which would enable them to familiarize themselves with the young prospects and give them major league instruction while playing in the minors.

Wrigley had understandably come to the conclusion that managers were needless figureheads. The Cubs had gone through seven managers since 1945 with zero success and the fans had apparently had enough since attendance figures were beginning to slump.

The Revolving Head Coach system came complete with an athletic director, Ret. Col. Robert Whitlow, who was supposed to hone the Cubs into a master race with a fierce exercise program. The Cubs were to arrive at the park at 0800 hours and do, oh, 800 wind sprints or so.

Whitlow was a military man who knew as much baseball as General Hooker (General Hooker gained his fame for indoor sports during the Civil War when he had an entourage of women follow his troops to relieve his men from the pressures of war). Col. Whitlow occasionally brought his spit shine and closely cropped hair in front of a microphone to mumble something about the Air Force diet and the necessity of strict discipline in developing good morale. But mostly, he hid in his Wrigley Field office where Cub fans figured he was devising a way to start World War III.

This was a confused, tumultous period for the Cub management and fans. For the ballplayers, however, it was business as usual. 60-94 in 1960 before Col. Bob and his ten corporals, 64-90 in 1961 and 59-103 in 1962. Pretty damn consistent. There was nothing the Cub organization could do to shake up this group. The Cubs knew they were on the right track since one of the trademarks of a championship team is its unflapability.

If the truth be known, the revolving head coaches did create instability. It just didn't mean much when the current head coach would say, "You're my regular centerfielder, you're going to have to play yourself out of the line-up" and four days later a new head coach would say the same thing to a different centerfielder.

There was no continuity to strategy. One head coach would like to hit and run, another would use the bunt and a third would snooze in the shade and ignore the game. One day a situation arose in the ballgame where a sign had to be flashed to the batter. A quick vote was taken after a long distance call to Tacoma. The vote count ended in a 5-5 tie and the third base coach called the batter aside and told him to do what he wanted.

It is traditional in baseball that a troubled ballplayer meets with the manager to discuss his problems. With the 61-62 Cubs, the players didn't know who to talk to. A perplexed Cub pitcher would approach the closed door of the manager's office, knock and ask "Who's there?" It was like tuning in the Tonight Show on a Monday to see who was filling in.

Confusion, Turmoil, Mayhem .... thy name is the Chicago Cubs.

Friedrich Durrenmatt, the Swiss author, wrote a short story entitled, "The Tunnel." The story dealt with a man who boarded a train. The man was calmly sitting in his cushioned seat looking at the scenery out of the window. The train rounded a curve into a tunnel. At first, this didn't affect the man, but as the tunnel got longer and longer, he became nervous. The man could no longer look out of the window since it was pitch dark in the tunnel. The man had taken this route before and remembered the tunnel but he never remembered it being this long. As the tunnel continued, the man got frightened. He wanted to see the bright daylight again. It seemed like they had been in the tunnel for hours. The tunnel continued and it became agonizing for the man. He was helpless; there was nothing he could do to stop the train from continuing in the tunnel and there was nothing he could do to shorten the tunnel. The tunnel never did end. It went on for infinity. The man's calm serene feelings as he entered the tunnel slowly turned to torturous panic.

Durrenmatt was writing the story of Cub fans who got aboard the pennant express after the 1945 season.

Leo Durocher once called Jack Brickhouse a "mental midget." Brickhouse, the father of the WGN sports family, was rightfully irked about this remark. Over six feet tall, Jack reasoned it was ridiculous to describe him as a midget in any terms.

As proof of his mental alertness, Brickhouse need only point to the high quality of humor and witticisms which are a trademark of his telecasts. The hilarity this jokester generates has thousands of viewers rolling on the floor in front of their television sets. The only other member of the WGN family in his company as a maker of merriment is his director, Arne Harris.

Brickhouse's comedic qualities are merely one facet of his many talents. He has gained his reputation through many years of competent description of sporting events. He has developed a remarkable interview technique which has enabled him to get interviews with both sports and political giants. Jack has a knack of never irritating his interviewee by disagreeing with him or asking him controversial questions ... or listening to what he says.

We must forgive Jack for never delving into the interviewee's character, personality, or opinion of significant events. We must also forgive Jack if occasionally he doesn't concentrate, as: "Tom, tell us a little about your background." Tom: "I was born in Cedar Rapids, Iowa, first played professionally with Pawtucket in Class B ball, etc." Jack: "Where did you first play professional ball?"

Mr. Durocher should be ashamed of himself for insulting Jack. Mr. Brickhouse has made mistakes, but this is only human.

Leo must have been watching the day the Cubs were playing the then Houston Colt 45's in Houston. The Cubs were winning by a run with one out and two men on base for Houston. One of the Houston players hit a line drive that clearly went between Billy Williams' outstretched glove and the Cubs' centerfielder and two runs scored. Brickhouse's account of what transpired went something like this: "There's a long fly. Run, Billy, Run! .... He's got it! What a catch! This one could have saved the game for the Cubbies!" Meanwhile, the stunned viewers at home saw Williams chasing the ball to the wall and two Houston players scampering around the bases. Later Brickhouse explained that there was a poor lighting system in the ballpark and from his vantage point it appeared as if Williams had caught the ball.

Leo must have also seen the White Sox-Tiger game years ago when Al Kaline of the Tigers hit a towering drive down the left field line and Brickhouse yelled at the top of his lungs, "Stay fair, Baby!" He had a little lapse and got the teams mixed up.

Maybe Leo saw the game between the Cubs and the Dodgers at Wrigley Field when the wind was blowing in from left field at a powerful clip and Frank Howard hit a long shot toward left. Brickhouse said, "Look out. That's hit. Wind or no wind, that's out of here." The next thing you know, Billy Williams is racing in toward home plate in a frantic attempt to catch the ball.

Leo might even have heard the Bear game in which the Bears were stopped on third down right at the goal line. For some reason Brickhouse thought they had scored and was yelling, "Touchdown, Touchdown!" When the Bears kicked a field goal on fourth down, Brickhouse thought it was the extra point and announced the score incorrectly for the next five minutes.

... Or heard him suggest an outfielder for Montreal might be given the take sign with two strikes on him.

... Or heard him do basketball games when every maneuver is described as the "old back door play."

... Or heard him describe the Chicago Mustangs soccer game, saying that names like Czechowicz and Przcykski would be household names in a few years.

Leo might have been listening on virtually thousands of occasions. But Leo, these were honest mistakes. These mistakes don't necessarily mean that Brickhouse has fewer brains than you or me. Personally, I would always choose Jack Brickhouse over Marcel Marceau to announce the big ball games, or as Mr. Brickhouse puts it, "The super crucial, pier six donnybrooks."

Jack Brickhouse is not the only comic relief for Chicago TV viewing fans. They have the commercials. The commercials between innings are so spell-binding that few fans can break away for the 60 second interlude to go to the bathroom. How could anyone leave the screen when in the space of a minute, right before his eyes, he can see Murph, the Union 76 dealer, try to convince us that truck stops are fine places to stage a special dinner party? Or he can watch the Schlitz bull demolish someone's new dining room set.

I was upset when they outlawed cigarette commercials on TV. I used to love the commercials with the sedate young lady singing about herself and her cigarettes who suddenly turns into a crazed nymphomaniac. Or the harmless cigarette package that lept out of the hands of a man-about-town and lurched drunkenly out of the city into the country. People are paying $3.00 to see action packed plots such as these at theatres across the country. Nightly I marvel at the luck of Chicago's baseball fans exposed to such one minute dramas free. Remember the "Winston tastes good as a cigarette should," as opposed to "Winston tastes good like a cigarette should" ads? Two or three times during every ballgame, they gave us free grammatical instruction. Bless these people. I went to Southern Illinois University and paid extravagant tuition fees for the English lessions I received. The ad asked the brainteaser: "What do you want, good grammar or good taste?" The magnitude of that question was too great to consider for 60 seconds. During a rain delay they should have had a panel discussion with Bergen Evans and S. I. Hayakawa on one side and Dean Martin and Jackie Gleason on the other. It would be satisfying to once and for all determine whether the American public wants good grammar or good taste.

Commonwealth Edison, one of the current sponsors, is beginning to burn my butt. They have also been sponsoring every other type of programming on TV as well. It is upsetting to me only if Commonwealth Edison is being charged for these advertisements. I suspect they are since I don't think a TV network would call up Com Ed and say "Why don't you fellows put something together telling us what's going on at the company and we'll telecast it to two million homes for you. Hey, of course, no charge. Just give us more than your usual half hour grace period if we are late with a payment before dousing our lights. It was damn embarrassing when you shut everything off before we could look behind door number three of our "big deal of the day" last week."

It bothers me if Com Ed must pay thousands of dollars for these ads because I assume in the long run, I and my fellow energy junkies are paying the tab. If Com Ed's operating expenses are higher, it doesn't figure that my electrical bill will be lower.

When it comes to public utilities, I don't know why they advertise. After all, it's not a matter of the consumer getting aggravated with their product and taking their business to Archie's Electricity or Kowalski's Gas and Light.

I wish they would drop that "working for you" routine. If they really are working for me, they could mail me a monthly profit check. And their "we're involved" slogan is only true if they are speaking of the booze they are pumping into legislators who sponsor bills favorable to Com Ed.

The fans should cry tilt! It's a new ballgame.

Astroturf is the silliest thing to happen to baseball since Bowie Kuhn became the Commissioner. It's a completely new event now. There are no more bunts; the Texas league single has become the Texas league triple; infielders become outfielders, since they are able to throw people out at first from short left field. Ground balls are hit directly to an infielder or get through to the outfield. Rod Carew would be the first .500 hitter if he played all his games on Astroturf. Balls get by outfielders for extra base hits with more regularity than senior citizens who take Serutan. Shit! Astroturf turns baseball into a giant pin ball game.

The St. Louis Cardinals, in the four game series over the July 4th weekend, became the pin ball wizards of the league. They must have hit ten Baltimore Choppers, topped balls that bounced so high that Lou Brock, Gary Templeton, Jerry Mumphrey and Tony Scott could get to Baltimore by the time they came down. The slower runners would only reach Indianapolis.

The Cardinals made me wonder if the Cubs have really changed. The eight and one half game lead the Cubs had when they arrived in St. Louis did not create a Robert E. Lee at Appomattox concession. The Cardinals resurrected the old bumbling style Cub fans have grown to tolerate. In one Busch stadium game, the Cubs made five errors in the first inning.

I refuse to blame the Cubs' ineptness on their ineptness. Astroturf is the culprit. The way the balls bounce here, the Cubs would have slaughtered them in basketball.

Baseball is a game that appeals to 75 year olds and ten year olds. It appeals to lawyers and bricklayers, to city boys and farm boys, to Mexicans and Canadians. No other sport has the same touch with the past. In baseball, players are revered even if they are best remembered for dropping a third strike, failing to touch second base or giving up an important home run. Fans remember utility infielders from 20 years ago. How many sports fans can name the reserve noseguard on the 1970 Cincinnati Bengals or even know what a noseguard is?

Fathers and sons can have a fun-filled outing together at the ballpark. Age doesn't make a difference, with the exception that if you are from a younger generation, you can expect to hear how much better the players were years ago than they are now. When I grew up, we were told how great Joe DiMaggio and Jimmy Fox were. The generation before me heard about Pie Traynor and Lou Gehrig; before that Babe Ruth and Ty Cobb.

I'll try not to tell my son how superior it was in my youth. He will know by comparing the names of the players of today with those of the fifties. We had Gus Zernial and Gus Triandos. He has Pepe Frias and Duffy Dyer. We had Turk Lown and Dutch Leonard. He has Wilbur Wood and Johnny Wockenfuss. We had Duke Snider and Ted Kluzewski. He has Nellie Briles and Robin Yount. We had Joe Adcock and Enos Slaughter. They have Enos Cabell and Ronny Blomberg. The fifties produced Moose Skowron and Jungle Jim

Rivera. Today we have Bucky Dent and Lenny Randle. The fifties had Rip Repulski and Jabber Jablonski. The modern players are Tippy Martinez and Cookie Rojas.

I think Clay Dalrymple's appearance in 1960 was the transition between the macho names of the fifties and the Casper Milquetoast names of today.

Following are a few of my lists for favorite groupings of ballplayers:

Ten Cubs Who Sound Like They Should Be Shoe Salesmen

1. George Gerberman 1962
2. Christopher Kitsos 1954
3. Arthur Ceccarelli 1959
4. Charles Hartenstein 1965
5. Harry Perkowski 1955
6. Frank Reberger 1968
7. Boots Day 1970
8. Wayne Terwilliger 1949
9. Bobby Tiefenauer 1968
10. Steve Bilko 1954

Ten Good Hit - No Field Cubs

1. Wes Covington 1966
2. Rico Carty 1973
3. Smoky Burgess 1949
4. Moose Moryn 1956
5. Ralph Kiner 1953
6. Hank Sauer 1949
7. Bill Madlock 1974
8. Willie Smith 1968
9. Clarence Jones 1967
10. Billy Williams 1959

Ten Good Field - No Hit Cubs

1. Jose Arcia 1968
2. Paul Popovich 1964
3. Ken Hubbs 1961
4. Don Kessinger 1964
5. Rob Sperring 1974
6. Ty Cline 1966
7. Jim Fanning 1954
8. Elvin Tappe 1954
9. Lee Elia 1968
10. Roger Metzger 1970

Ten Cubs of Italian Ancestry

1. Dom Dallessandro 1940
2. Ken Aspromonte 1963
3. Joey Amalfitano 1964
4. Chris Canizzaro 1971
5. Tony Larussa 1973
6. Vito Valentinetti 1956
7. Phil Cavaretta 1934
8. Ernie Broglio 1964
9. Bob Ramazotti 1949
10. Juan Pizarro 1970

Ten Cub Pitchers With Hanging Curveballs

1. Wayne Schurr 1964
2. Bob Anderson 1957
3. Tom Dettore 1974
4. John Buzhardt 1958
5. Darcy Fast 1968
6. Paul Toth 1962
7. Jim Todd 1974
8. Hy Cohen 1955
9. Don Kaiser 1955
10. Dave Lemonds 1969

Ten Cubs We Couldn't Trade For A Baseball Bat

1. Jimmy Qualls 1969

2. Earl Averill 1959
3. Gene Hiser 1971
4. Ellis Burton 1963
5. Don Young 1965
6. Hector Torres 1971
7. Bobby Gene Smith 1962
8. Mel Roach 1961
9. Jerry Kindall 1956
10. Cleo James 1970

Ten Most Forgettable Cub Players

1. Billy Cowan 1963
2. Andre Rodgers 1961
3. Jim King 1955
4. Jim Bolger 1955
5. Don Landrum 1962
6. Sterling Slaughter 1964
7. Norm Gigon 1967
8. Len Gabrielson 1964
9. Steve Boros 1963
10. Don Hoak 1956

Ten Cubs Who Never Lived Up to Press Clippings (Underachievers)

1. Dick Drott 1957
2. Moe Drabowsky 1956
3. Lee Gregory 1964
4. Solly Drake 1956
5. Bob Speake 1955
6. Chris Ward 1972
7. Lou Brock 1961
8. Gary Ross 1968
9. Nelson Mathews 1960
10. Adolfo Phillips 1966

My Ten Favorite Cubs (Don't Ask Me Why)

1. Ernie Banks 1953
2. Andy Pafko 1943

3. Eddie Miksis 1951
4. Jimmy Stewart 1963
5. Frankie Baumholtz 1949
6. George Altman 1959
7. Lindy McDaniel 1963
8. Phil Regan 1968
9. Bob Buhl 1962
10. Tony Taylor 1958

Ten Over-The-Hill Players With The Cubs

1. Robin Roberts 1966
2. Lew Burdette 1964
3. Ralph Kiner 1953
4. Bobby Thompson 1958
5. Don Larsen 1967
6. Dick Radatz 1967
7. Bobby Shantz 1964
8. Richie Ashburn 1960
9. Ed Bailey 1965
10. Frank Thomas 1960

A Cubbie breakdown can happen to anyone. It strikes the young or elderly, developing as a fan becomes overly involved in any Cubs' game.

Minds and bodies can only stand so much punishment. The fans who constantly get upset at the goings-on in the ballgame often are overtaxing their systems and are prone to an attack.

From my experience, an unwritten agreement has been drawn up between a man's emotional make-up and his physical system. Most systems, being sturdy, can accept violent outbursts at appropriate times during a ballgame. Even the less hardy systems would endure a fan reacting in an overly vigorous manner when their team commits a crucial error in a pressure-packed situation. The systems sustain the fan who occasionally gets upset when a manager or player uses questionable strategy.

But the systems are overtaxed by fans who become upset prematurely in a game or who go wild for no apparent justifiable reason.

I got a call at home today. Smitty had had a Cubbie breakdown.

Smitty asked too much of his system while watching the games. He was taking advantage of his good health.

He invited me over to his house for one of the games against the Phillies. He was alright during the Philly half of the first, but I could see something was wrong with him when the Cubs batted. DeJesus led off and took a strike. "What's he waiting for?" my friend screamed. "The pitch was right down the middle." On the next pitch DeJesus lunged for a low, outside, fast ball. "What's he helping the pitcher out for?" my friend yelled. "He's the lead-off man. He should be taking pitches." On and on it went, pitch after pitch.

When Trillo booted a ball with two out and no one on, my friend's face turned purple with rage. Every time Philly had the tying man at the plate he had to excuse himself while he took a pill. He broke a beer bottle over a chair when an umpire called a close one against the Cubs. After I saw this, I knew I had to get out of the house as quickly as possible.

I slipped out when my friend went to vomit between the fourth and fifth innings. Later, after the call, I visited him in the hospital. Even though he recognized me, I knew he was gone. I asked him how he was feeling. He said, "It was right down the middle, damn it. Swing away for chrissakes. Put Steve Swisher up there, Franks."

I didn't bother to slip out. I just turned around and ran. The Cubbie breakdown had claimed another victim.

All baseball announcers have a common problem. They have to keep their audience even during the late innings in a 10-1 game.

On the old Truth or Consequences show a contestant would be given the opportunity to win prizes by placing a telephone call to a name picked at random out of the phone book and keeping the party in a conversation for three minutes. It wasn't an easy assignment. There is a hesitancy about talking to strangers.

Contestants who are able to keep a conversation going with people who have no idea who they're talking to are entertaining people or master salesmen. Most of us couldn't do it. Luckily for most of us, we never run across such a challenge in our professional or personal lives.

But the livelihood of hundreds of announcers across the country depends on their ability to keep people listening to idle chatter. You might think, "It's not difficult. They've got the sport working for them. Everyone listens to the ballgame anyway."

Usually this is true. But is there anything more boring than a one-sided athletic contest? Suppose the Los Angeles Dodgers jump out to an 8-0 lead against the Houston Astros in the fourth inning and the Dodgers have Don Sutton pitching. If you're an Astro fan, the radio knob is going to be turned counter-clockwise. Even the most faithful fan can't take too many high pop-ups and grounders to short. If you have shut off the radio, who will be listening to the sponsors' messages?

Think about the team that loses 100 ballgames a year. There are going to be many games which they are out of by the sixth inning. The sponsor won't look sympathetically towards the radio announcer. He'll assume the announcer just doesn't have enough appeal for the listening audience and maybe a change would help sales.

The next time you're watching a 4-0 game in the ninth inning with two outs in which your team has only managed one hit off Tom Seaver, don't be offended if the announcer says, "Now if only Jones can get an infield hit and then Smith in the on-deck circle can draw a walk and Jackson in the hole can line a single and Simpson at the end of the bench representing the tying run can hit one off the wall and Johnson now making wee-wee in the clubhouse can smash a home run, we'll have won the game." The announcer is just trying to keep the meat and potatoes on his family's dinner table.

As for my meat and potatoes, it's hard to keep 'em down when listening to that drivel.

The 1947 to 1967 Cub years were leaner than Cher. They never won a game they should have lost in that span.

Buzz Lewin, a fan who rarely missed a Cub error in the past 20 years recalls the wretched seasons ... "It was a peaceful time ... those years. You could doze off in the sun and only occasionally be awakened by the sound of bat on ball or a foul slamming onto an empty seat next to you. The bleacher bums weren't an organized bunch then. Oh, sure, there were bums in those days, but they came to the park only to avoid being picked up on loitering charges. The Cubs' advertising campaign centered on beautiful Wrigley Field with the green grass and vines and the chance to be outdoors with your friends. 'Bring a lunch and have a picnic' they used to say. At the very end of the commercial they added, 'and see a major league baseball game, too'. Yes, it was a different way of life for Cub fans then."

"The game was a simpler one for most Cub fans in the 40's and 50's. Today when we go to games we know the Cubs can either win, lose, or the game might be called because of darkness. In the old days, we knew the Cubs would either lose or the game might be called because of darkness."

The main thing I remember about the 60's was the army reserve and ballplayers being taken away for two weeks at a time just when the team was planning to come out of a three-game losing streak. I remember one time when Don Kessinger received a weekend pass from his army camp in Kansas. He flew to Los Angeles and won a game for them with a double. If it were the 50's, the player would have been Ed Bouchee, and they would have rushed him to the park in time to commit two fatal errors in the ninth inning. Or he would have flown to New York and found out the Cubs were in Philadelphia. I don't even remember what the army was doing in the fifties. All I knew was Cowboys and Indians.

The 70's have been kinder. The Cubs actually had seasons when they won more games than they lost. This all, no doubt, is building up toward three or four consecutive world championships. I'd settle for one.

Cub fans generally hibernate in the winter. Only those fans who slip on the ice are reminded of the Cubs. The others mutter "wait until next year" and happily yell their lungs out at Bear and Bull games for five months.

This year the winter siesta was interrupted by the shocking trades of Madlock and Monday: Bill Madlock, the young third baseman who had just won back-to-back National League batting championships; Rick Monday, their leading home run hitter, best defensive outfielder and a fellow Pat Boone would allow to date his daughters.

Fans weren't shocked that the Cubs wanted some trades. When you finish fifth out of six teams the biggest shake-up can only drop you one spot in the standings.

Stupid trades are what concerned the fans. To begin with, Chicago Cub fans are always suspicious of any kind of deals. To this day the leaves of the sumacs around the ballpark whisper, "Ernie Broglio, Ernie Broglio." Broglio was, of course, the sore-armed pitcher the Cubs acquired by trading future Hall of Famer, Lou Brock.

So when Cub fans learned the Cubs had traded Rick Monday and reliever Mike Garman for Bill Buckner and his gimpy foot, an untested near rookie shortstop, Ivan DeJesus, and minor league pitcher, Jeff Albert, many of them reported a theft to the Chicago police. And when 25 year old batting champion Bill Madlock and infielder Rob Sperring were traded to the Giants for 30 year old

Bobby Murcer coming off a poor year, ne'er-before-do-well Steve Ontiveros and minor league pitcher Andy Muhlstock, Cub fans were outraged.

Trades, of course, are determined by whether the climate of the city will agree with the new player, whether the salary requirements will be above or below a million dollars, whether the player's agent's personality is compatible with management and whether the Chinese laundry down the street will agree to clean and press the incoming player's jock straps. But even then, these trades simply did not make sense.

We were wrong. So far in 1977 the Cubs are ecstatic with the results of the two major off-season trades. Those fans who abandoned ship after they were announced are now eating crow, but if we wind up in first place, the crow will taste delicious.

Wrigley Field has a traffic and parking problem that has kept even an addict like myself home on days I can't cope with bedlam. Especially on Sundays. I sympathize with people who are fed up with their programmed lives of Monday through Friday. But why can't they escape to the solitude of the Iowa cornfields instead of cluttering the Chicago lakefront? Everyone and his out-of-town cousin are on Lake Shore Drive on Sundays. Haven't they ever seen water before?

The Cubs play at noon when they have Sunday double-headers. If I leave home at ten, I get there at 12:15. If I leave at nine, I still get there at 12:15. It frustrates me to arrive at a sporting event after the game has started. Part of the excitement is the anticipation of the event, peaking and culminating at the first play. I hate being late and I blame bikinis and Schwinns and orangutans and cops and Puerto Ricans and taxi drivers. Let me explain.

I know all about Sunday drivers. When I was a child my Dad would cuss the goddamn Sunday drivers. I thought he was kidding, but now I realize there are people who use their car only to visit Aunt Matilda in Wilmette on Sunday. Because of these additional drivers, there are traffic jams and more accidents on the day God told everyone to rest.

Before I even get to the loop from my south suburban home, I have hit 29 red lights, ten pot-holes and have averaged 16 m.p.h. Since Lake Shore Drive's speed limit is 45 m.p.h. and I'm going 16, I feel I have 29 m.p.h. coming to me.

I get by the loop, take the extra 29 m.p.h. and am doing 74 as I approach the Oak Street Beach. Hell if I'm going to do 74 past 10,000 two piece bathing suits. Thirty minutes and thousands of beautiful bodies later, I'm running late.

I reach Fullerton, the least congested exit to Wrigley Field. There are only eight cars in front of me. I inch my way to the stop sign. I'm ready to accelerate when a cyclist cruises in front of me ... then another ... and another ... a fourth ... fifth ... twelfth ad infinitum. All I see are spinning spokes, inverted handlebars, high seats and helmets. Fat people, slim ones, males and females all doing their macho thing on my day at Wrigley. Alright, a blow-out and through the opening I slither only to run into the happy, leisurely Lincoln Park Zoo crowd. They amble in front of my car carrying their binoculars and National Geographics like a herd of lumbering buffalo. God damn it, I've got a ballgame to get to. One of them drops their bag of peanuts, my foot hits the gas pedal and I zoom through the amber light only to hear the dulcet tones of a Chicago police car's siren. How the hell did the cop get by the cyclists and zoologists?

"Let's see your license."
"What did I do?"
"Ran a red light. You got a bond card?"
"No."

Ten minutes and a ticket later, I'm on my way cursing myself for not keeping a $20.00 bill under my license like Luigi does. Cops gotta eat too.

Finally, I can see Wrigley Field and hell if that's not a parking spot just a block away. I stop and start to back in. There's a rap at the window and a bearded man says, "Hey, MON, what you doin'? Don you see my chair sittin' there?" Sure enough there is a chair where a car ought to be. "I'm savin' the spot, amigo. You don park here." I still have nightmares from the street fight scenes from West Side Story, so I proceed.

But now there are no parking spots anywhere, legal or illegal. The few parking lots around Wrigley Field look like the Dan Ryan Expressway. I can't chance parking my car on private property since Lincoln Towing Company would claim it and to get it back, it would cost $50.00 and my first born male child.

Another 15 minutes and I find a nice little spot three miles from the park. A definite cab ride. I flag down a Checker and holler,

"Wrigley Field!"

"I'm not about to go there, I'll be stuck an hour and can't get no fare back before the game."

"Come on, I'll give you a big tip."

"How big?"

"just drive, god damn it."

Another 15 minutes and I race into the park, and gape at the scoreboard. Second inning, 6-0 Astros, AAAAAAARGH!!!!!!!

Cub Fan: "Hey, I don't want to hear about it. They're in the American League."

Sox Fan: "What the hell does that mean?"

Cub Fan: "That means I put the American League with the League of Women Voters, the Patrolmens' League and 20,000 Leagues under the Sea. They all have nothing to do with baseball."

Sox Fan: "How come Rich Gossage, Jeff Burroughs, and George Hendricks are burning up the National League? And how come the Cubs got shut out by an American League castoff, Jackie Brown, the other day?"

Cub Fan: "Why is Larry Hisle, who bounced around the National League, driving in runs like Hank Greenberg used to? Why do you think they call it the Junior Circuit?"

Sox Fan: "Let's get to the point. The Cubs smell. They have the most embarrassing record in baseball history."

Cub Fan: "Yeah, except for the Sox who went 40 years without winning the pennant."

Sox Fan: "Well, if the Cubs don't win the pennant this year, I'm sure they'll surpass 40. I've always said they would never win in my lifetime."

Cub Fan: "It would be just like you to slash your wrists the day before they clinch it to make that statement come true."

Sox Fan: "Let's go position by position. I'll prove the Sox are better. At first we got Spencer and Lamar Johnson. That beats Buckner."

Cub Fan: "I'm not conceding but keep going."

Sox Fan: "At second, I'll take Orta over Trillo."

Cub Fan: "You're full of shit. Orta couldn't catch a cold."

Sox Fan: "Bannister and DeJesus are a draw at short. I'll take Soderholm over Ontiveros at third. I'll take Essian over any of your catchers. Zisk over your left fielder. I'll give you Morales and Murcer in center and right. So it's Sox 5, Cubs 2 and 1 draw."

Cub Fan: "You are out of your mind. How about pitching? That's only 90 percent of the game. And the Sox bench can't compare with the Cubs. And you don't have the team speed, the defense, the versatility, the team character ... "

Sox Fan: "Yeah, I know. The Cubs are the greatest."

Cub Fan: "Furthermore, the Cubs have better fans and security at their ballpark. There aren't one-tenth the fights and drunken beer parties at Wrigley Field. Wrigley Field is far prettier, we have grilled hot dogs, our scoreboard is better, we have prettier usherettes, cleaner restrooms and nicer scorecards."

Sox Fan: "We have a better organist and more parking."

Cub Fan: "You're full of shit."

Change a few names around and the argument could have taken place in 1906 (the last time the Cubs played the Sox in the World Series), 1935, 1955, 1975 or tomorrow.

The only good thing about the White Sox is that a Sox game was the scene of my first sexual triumph.

The date was June 1, 1956. I was a fifth grader and the White Sox were playing Boston. My date was Jill Goodman, a girl with a ponytail halfway down her back and a smirk on her face. She knew that I was scared stiff. I hadn't planned to go on my first date until my honeymoon.

This whole thing came about when one of the early developers in class, the type of kid who had to give up cigarettes because he was coming down with lung cancer, thought a fitting end to the school year would include a boy-girl group outing to Sox park.

We had about a two week warning. Each night, I fell into a troubled sleep knowing that tomorrow would be the day I should ask someone to go with me. If I didn't make my move soon, I would end up with Phyliss Diller Jr. and lose my high standing on the nicotine breath list.

The days passed and all the girls I had a crush on were snatched up by the time I had the nerve to clear my throat. Possibly even worse than a date with a girl whose features were unusually arranged was a rejection. To this day, I have trouble handling a rejection. I wasn't too happy when my Army classification was 1-Y.

Jill was the only girl left who could pass as a human being, and I popped the question. She laughed for one solid minute before accepting.

We all met at the home of a kid who volunteered his mother to drive. The chain smoking kid's car was in the shop.

Jill and I nodded and promptly began a period of silence longer than the one between the USA and Red China. Marlon Brando was my hero then, and I attempted to emulate him by talking in two-word sentences and making an occasional animal grunt.

At the ballgame, I tried to buy her affections, but all I got my hands on were five hot dogs, one cotton candy, and three frosty malts.

On top of it, the Sox won handily. The Cubs, whose talents I had been espousing all day, were being decimated in Cincinnati 14-0.

On the way home, I managed to hold Jill's hand and was content knowing I had scored better than the Cubs.

Some people do their jobs too well, like the Wrigley Field ushers. On those occasions when I splurge on a box seat, it's my habit to switch seats at regular intervals. I generally start from my actual seat way down the foul lines and about 25 rows back (the seat I got from the crooked box office people despite writing in four months in advance) and by the sixth inning, I've worked my way up to the first three rows behind one of the dugouts.

The proper technique is to spot some empty seats in the prestige sections and watch them for two innings. If no one has claimed them by then, you wait for the next half inning to end, then you swagger past the authorities to the promised land. In previous years this plan would come off like clockwork. It was nothing to get by the 16 year old Andy Frain boys. But so many people were following my formula, the ballpark hired 16 year old Andy Frain girls or usherettes or SS Gestapo women. Since the usherettes, I never feel safe in my fraudulently obtained seats. I know that at any time during any inning, there could come a tap on my shoulder and the accusing, "Do you have a ticket for this seat?" I sit there for an additional ten seconds, glower at the female authority figure and then sheepishly crawl back to my original seat until it's time to make my next move.

These young girls bug me. They indiscriminately go through the box seat section and ask people whether they have tickets for their seats. I can understand this when the actual ticket owners arrive or in the case of a rowdy individual. But it is totally uncalled for when a young boy with a grandstand ticket and finally in the ninth inning after some people have left has a chance to sit near his heroes. Or in the case of a box seat holder who has paid the same price for his ticket as do the people who sit right behind the dugout and who has moved into obviously unoccupied seats.

I have devised my own system for retaliating against these attacks. I ask people who are leaving luxury seats for their ticket stubs. Now I just love it when one of these bitches taps me on the shoulder.

I can sense when they are approaching and simultaneously with their shoulder tap, I snap my head around and snarl, "What do you want?" Undaunted, they say, "Do you have a ticket for this seat?" I say "None of your business." They say, "It is my business. It's my job to find out." I don't say another word, nor do I give any indication that she's still there. I keep my eyes on the ballgame until finally, partly because she doesn't know what to do and partly because the other fans are hollering "Sit down, sister," she retreats.

Two minutes later a 16 year old male Andy Frain will appear. He says, "Sir, if you don't have a ticket for this seat, you'll have to move." The girl is smirking in the background. "I ain't movin," I growl.

Both of them leave and come back with the head usher (a 17-year-old with a white hat). He's always a little bigger than the 16 year old and he says, "Sir, you'll have to come along with me." I say, "Just a minute. What is your name?"

He says, "Billy Oldman."

I say, "And what are the names of the young girl and boy?"

They say, "Harry Hischool and Bertha Brickhead."

Then I **really** get tough. "I have never experienced such harassment and incompetent service as I have received today. You may rest assured a scathing letter will be sent to your superiors about your inconsiderate behavior."

Then I produce my ticket stub. I demand personal apologies from all concerned and send them on their way, happy with the knowledge that Bertha Brickhead will be a little more leery about whom she picks on the next time.

If the Frain brigade really wanted to maintain tranquility, they should trade Bertha Brickhead and Harry Hischool for Helmut Punter, an usher from a Prussian Ushering Service who once kicked four people in the head during a soccer melee between Butzbach and Kaiserslautern.

When the Cubs are away from home, it's like a respiratory case leaving his oxygen tent. The club is as insecure as an obese third grader on the first day at a new school. Rightfully so. The road record through the years has been putrid. As Casey Stengel used to say, "You can look it up." The worst thing about road games has always been the ballparks: the older they are the worse they are.

Take Pittsburgh's Forbes Field. I see visions of Roberto Clemente circling the bases like a berserk animal in the bottom of the ninth. I see Matty Alou chopping down on the ball and hitting a high bounder off the cement-like infield over the third baseman's head. I see Ernie Banks connecting with that sweet swing and to hit a towering drive that is in the 3rd row seats at Wrigley Field, but is still a full 30 feet from the fence in Pittsburgh. I see Cub batters swinging futilely at Dock Ellis' pitches even though I know Ellis would be lucky to hold them to 12 runs in Chicago. I *don't* see the left fielder, center fielder, right fielder, or anything in the outfield — I didn't then — the lighting was too weak. I *did* see far too many Cub losses in that Chamber of Horrors.

Crosley Field's demise in Cincinnati wasn't such a sad affair either. This was the only park that had an incline for a warning track. The Cincinnati players knew it, the Phillies, Cardinals, Dodgers, Pirates, Giants and Braves also knew it. The Cub outfielders always reacted as if there had been a shifting of the earth precisely when they were trying to corner a fly ball. They'd back up against the wall, pound their glove and ... start rolling down the hill like a runaway sled.

Ebbets Field and the Polo Grounds were more like amusement parks than baseball stadiums to the Cubs. They'd sit back in awe watching the baseballs bounce merrily every which way off the acute angles of the park.

Philadelphia's old park was affectionately known as the cow pasture because of its uneven landscape. The Cubs seemed to be expecting cow pies the way they tip-toed around the field.

I refuse to discuss the Astrodome in Houston, other than mentioning that everything imaginable has gone wrong there, including a rain delay despite the domed roof.

Take me back home to the friendly confines where a wind blown home run is a wind blown home run.

A few years ago, I followed the Cubs down to St. Louis one weekend. I had the entire trip planned for weeks in advance. Yet, after the Cubs lost 2-0 in the opening night game of this weekend series, I considered abandoning my plans. The 2-0 loss was so frustrating that I had lost my interest in driving the 300 miles to St. Louis. I figured, even if they won Saturday, they'd be just as well off as they were before they lost Friday. This is faulty thinking. Every game you win counts.

So, I left at 4:00 a.m. Saturday morning, heading south. It is about a six-hour ride. I planned on getting in at about ten to look around a few hours before game time.

It took me 16 hours to get to St. Louis. My car was moving right along at 70 m.p.h. when it threw a rod and lay dead by the side of the road. I spent ten hours in Staunton, Illinois, whose projected population within three years is 5,000. The city hall is on top of the Dairy Queen, and people sit around speculating how exciting spending Saturday night in Granite City, Illinois would be.

The 1965 Dodge Dart that threw a rod 40 miles from St. Louis would have cost $300.00 to repair, so I sold the car for $50.00, but not until I listened to the Cardinal broadcasters describe the Cubs' loss on the radio.

I packed my license plate in my traveling bag, caught one of the infrequent Greyhound busses which slow down to pick up passengers, and we zig-zagged our way to St. Louis in a little less than three hours.

Arriving in St. Louis, I caught a cab to the Chase Park Plaza hotel where I had made reservations. Coincidentally, the Cubs were also staying there.

I registered and boarded the elevator along with Hank Aguirre and Ron Santo. Santo was carrying some crazy drink which looked like green glue. Aguirre uttered a few profanities to a bleacher bum who kept opening the elevator door just before it shut.

Santo had a key in his hand to Room 3208, which I quickly memorized. After unpacking, I headed for Room 3208. I could have found the room blindfolded. Music was blaring and the number of people would have eclipsed a Sunday crowd at White Sox park.

There was a sign on the door which read, "You must be 21 to enter." Having passed this only prerequisite, I entered. There were wall-to-wall people inside, all sipping Stag beer.

Although I don't want to go down in the annals of history as a stoolie, the ballplayers in attendance were Ron Santo, Hank Aguirre, Bill Hands, Randy Hundley, Willie Smith and Glenn Beckert.

Nothing especially incriminating took place although, I can assure you, the midnight curfew was blatantly violated. The players were lucky to get six hours sleep.

The fans had a good time with the players. Hank Aguirre led them in a dance known as "The

Leo" in which the gestures made are similar to the one Durocher once made to umpire Tony Venzon.

The Cubs lost the ballgame the following day by a score of 4-3. Was partying the key to the loss? Well, Aguirre, Hands and Hundley didn't get in the game. Santo got two hits and played beautifully in the field, Willie Smith was one for one as a pinchhitter and Beckert got a base hit and played errorless ball. And so, yet another theory dies.

The outstanding feature of this year's schedule is that the Cubs had no April games in Montreal. Since Montreal came into the league, the Cubs have always had an early season series in Canada. These games should be moved to a warmer climate, like Nome, Alaska. The schedule makers don't believe what they read in the papers or hear in the forecasts. Using new math, they divide the heat of the center of the sun (36,000,000°F) into the distance between Montreal and the sun (93,000,000 miles) and arrive at a predicted 55°. These guys could divide three into nine and get 55°. The fact is, bears still hibernate during April in Montreal. The early season games get played in 38° temperatures, give or take an icicle. Everyone has a fine time except the Cubs and the ice cream vendor. The Montreal pitchers throw snowballs instead of curveballs (Cub hitters don't make enough contact in these early season games to notice). Even George Mitterwald has no problem sliding in Montreal.

I don't mean to belittle Montreal or their fans. They have been a tremendous addition to baseball. When the weather warms up to partly freezing they have 30,000 enthusiastic Canadian rooters at their games. Ballplayers really enjoy playing for the Montreal people.

Since the Expos have come into being, the ballclub has been lousy. Their best offense has been their weather. French-Canadians are sly people, smuggling cold temperatures past U.S. Customs officials and bringing them to Chicago.

I became a charter member of the Cub's Polar Bear Club one day at a Cub/Expo game, when I arrived at the park two hours before game time. I had warned Smitty, who accompanied me, to dress extra warm. I suggested gloves, two pairs of socks, a sweater and a blanket. He laughed at my suggestion; I backed off and neither of us took my advice. That day I would have gladly traded the royalties from this book for a blanket. The teeny-boppers who came to the park in jerseys and cut-offs resembled grape popsicles by the seventh inning.

The Cubs don't play well in this type of weather. (I still haven't determined what type of weather they do play well in.) On this particular day, time after time, the Montreal pitcher (Stan Bahnsen) would shoot a hard one on the fists of a Cub slugger, placing a queen bee in the handle of their bats. The Cubs hit weak taps to the infielders and retreated to the dugout like baby bruins with buckshot in their hides.

Harry Caray's coke-bottle bottomed glasses indicate he can't see too well from his perch in the pressbox behind home plate. Yet, periodically, he insists on taking his myopia out to the centerfield bleachers to originate his broadcast. From centerfield, Lamar Johnson looks white to Harry.

The reason Harry does a remote from the bleachers is because he likes to promote the "one of the fans" image. What fan was ever roped off from his peers by 20 square feet? Do we have group halitosis?

White Sox fans don't seem to care if Caray has a common cold, syphilis or leprosy. They just want to mingle with their fuhrer and happily sit on their haunches wildly honking out his name on command.

Recently Harry had a special treat for us. Irv Kupcinet, freshly dismissed as Jack Brickhouse's color man on the Bears games and yearning to put in his two cents somewhere, accompanied Harry to the bleacher microphone. The byplay went something like this:

"Kup, it's great to have you out here. You can't beat fun at ..."

"Yeah, I know Jack. I've heard you say that before."

"Kup, you really look swell. Here, have a beer."

Kup, sitting in a sport coat and tie in the 90° heat, didn't feel too swell; "Thanks, Jack."

In the fourth inning Harry finally started to zero in on the game.

"We're going into the fourth. This game has been dull up to now ... but there goes Miss Chicago walking by."

Kup asks, "Where, Jack?"

Caray continues: "It's 3-0 on Rodney Scott. Come on Barrios. Put the ball in there. This guy can't hit."

Kup says, "Dat's right, Jack."

After three more innings, three more Jacks and six more beers, Harry explodes, "It's Harry, Kup. Harry! Haireeee!"

Kup fashions himself as a renaissance man, and they didn't have much baseball in the fifteenth century. Apparently getting a man's name right wasn't important then, either.

Last year, I was watching John Candalaria of the Pirates pitch a no-hitter on television. My excitement grew with each hitless inning. The game went into the ninth and my palms began to sweat. I needed to share the nervousness of the moment with someone, but I was home alone with Numi, the dog. Candalaria's masterpiece did nothing for her. The ninth inning was just beginning when my wife, Diane, came in with two bags of groceries.

"Diane, get in here quick," I screamed. She rushed into the room, spilling a cantaloupe en route.

"You got to watch. This is special. The Candy Man has a no-hitter going."

To Diane, a special is a seven-piece iced tea set for $3.99.

"Is that what you called me in for?"

"Yeah, watch. It's the ninth inning. The Dodgers haven't got a hit."

Just then, Davey Lopes hit a grounder to short and Diane announced, "There goes the no-hitter."

"What do you mean there goes the no-hitter? That's a ground-out to short."

"But he hit the ball. Why do they call it a no-hitter if he hit it?"

"You mean to tell me you've watched 100 games with me and don't know what a hit is yet?"

"Well, we've been listening to Brickhouse do the games. How do you expect me to know?" She had a point.

Sizemore hit a foul fly to right which was caught for the second out. "That's two gone," I hollered. "The Bucs can send their firemen and relief ace home and close up the bullpen. The Candy Man has his breaking pitch going. Did you see that roundhouse curve? Mixing it up with the hummer. No wonder he's got a super e.r.a. Who's on deck? Unless it's a utility man, give him a free pass. I hope if they get a hit, it's a frozen rope. None of those Texas leaguer's or carpet hits."

Diane looked at me as if I was speaking Swahili. The only thing that made any sense to her was the e.r.a.

Bill Russell glanced in the dugout half expecting a pinch-hitter. When none was forthcoming, he stepped in the batter's box and hit a high, long, foul fly. Strike one.

Diane wanted to know why Russell could keep batting after hitting a foul when Sizemore was out on his foul.

I told her Parker had caught Sizemore's foul and this was fair. A foul ball not caught is a strike. With two strikes on him, Russell hit a foul.

Diane didn't understand why I wasn't getting excited. "That was the third strike wasn't it? An uncaught foul ball is a strike. There were two strikes on the hitter. The game's over."

Wrongo, clever wife. I'm glad she didn't ask why a ball hitting the foul pole is fair and what a high fly to left has to do with a can of corn.

Russell flew to Oliver in center. Al Michaels announced Candalaria had pitched a no-hitter but not a perfect game.

Diane wanted me to explain why a no-hitter wasn't a perfect game. I wanted two aspirins. The excitement of the game and explaining terminology to her had created a throb. I yelled, "It's not worth explaining. Go buy a book and figure it out for yourself."

She did and can now rattle off the 13 ways a pitcher can commit a balk. Better barefoot and pregnant!

When the Cubs come home from losing road trips, their plane can arrive at O'Hare at 4:42 pm or 5:37 or 6:11. It doesn't matter, because people stay home in hordes. There are no banners, no red carpets, and no ticker tape parades. The wives usually send their maids to greet the losers at the airport.

When the Cubs have a successful road trip, a crowd from anywhere between 200 and 2000 is at the airport to greet the conquering heroes. These fanatic fans have autograph book and camera in hand waiting for the few glorious moments they can spend with the Cubs before the players dash off to their suburban homes.

Airport officials keep first aid supplies handy to treat the inevitable casualties. If the plane is two minutes behind schedule, an emotional sort will always gasp, "The plane's late. Something must have happened to them," as she tumbles to the ground. Smelling salts for her.

Then there are the injuries caused when someone screams, "There's Herman." About 600 people start trampling one another as they charge 100 yards toward a perplexed, petrified man whose only resemblance to Franks is that he's fat and balding. Splints and a stretcher for him.

Seconds later a crowd gathers around Joe Wallis or a person they believe to be Joe Wallis, who spends the next 15 minutes kissing girls and signing autographs, only to take off when the Cub plane actually arrives. Hemlock for him.

Cub players have tried to avoid the crowds by being delivered in foot lockers to the luggage area and by trying to slink by the crowds dressed in stewardess uniforms. Only Peanuts Lowrey, Rick and Paul Reuschel got by undetected last time.

The players have made a game of trying to get through the Cub fans' receiving line. The one who gets by with the least number of abrasions wins. The fans in turn try to pummel the players. They award each other 50 points for hitting Franks on his bald pate, hitting a Reuschel in his pizza belly, or pulling Morales' sideburns. Twenty-five points are given for ripping anyone's clothes and five points for drawing blood.

Too often the players are able to run around the frenzied fans. The fans have a shoddy defense. They fail to force the player to go up the middle and allow him to get to the outside. The fans should study game films of the Bears specialty teams. On second thought, they probably already have.

I don't condone all this violence, but after 32 years of losing, maybe the players owe the fans a piece of their scalps.

The final month of the season is a testing period for next season, the time to experiment with rookie prospects, except for pennant contenders, where no rookies will be in evidence. The regulars on these lucky teams will be playing day in and day out, rarely seeing a day of rest. Pennant contenders could probably get along with 18 men. The last seven men on a team don't figure to get in an "important" game.

Why do ballclubs keep three utility infielders and washed-up relief pitchers on their rosters during the crucial stretch of the season? These players just get in the way. It's even worse if the benchwarmer is a serious sort who adds to the tension as the season goes down to the wire.

All of which raises an interesting theory. Instead of having these Mickey the Mope ballplayers sitting in the dugout, why not at least put someone on the bench who is adept at keeping his teammates "loose" so that they'll be able to perform to their fullest capacities? Get a funnyman to keep the guys' minds off the seriousness of the game. Get somebody who, if he can't actually help his team by his athletic prowess, can at least stymie the opponents by needling them. Get somebody who will enhance his team's chances by his mere presence and warm personality. Get somebody like Don Rickles.

Just think how he could unnerve the opposition. Greg Luzinski steps up to the plate for the Phils in a clutch situation. His concentration rests solely on the Cub pitcher who is trying to get him out. Suddenly from the Cub dugout, Luzinski hears:

"Hey, dummy. You're too stupid to get a hit. I know you were born stupid, but I'm sorry for your recent relapse. You're like an old stove ... big belly and no head."

Luzinski glares towards the dugout, but the assault continues:

"Seriously, Greg, next time you pass my house, I'll appreciate it. Let's play horse. I'll be the front end — you just be yourself. Don't you ever get tired of having yourself around? Look, there's a train pulling out shortly — get under it."

Luzinski growls angrily at the Cub dugout. The benchwarmer continues:

"Why don't you sue your brains for non-support? Only your varicose veins keep you from being completely colorless. Why don't you go to the drugstore and get loaded on scotch tape? I don't know what makes you tick, but I hope it's a time bomb. You give the type of performance that gives failure a bad name."

The count reaches 0-2.

"Hey, Luzinski, you're in a hole more often than a gravedigger. The only thing you ever achieved on your own is dandruff. You're lucky you're not a building. You'd be condemned. I hear the Phillies are going to rent you out to a near-sighted knife thrower."

The pitcher fires a third fast one past the stunned batter.

On second thought, the Cubs always have had enough comedians on their teams.

I wish the Women's Lib

movement would move out of the newspapers. Everytime they picket Playboy magazine, crash an all male drinking pub or demand presents on Father's Day, they get a headline.

Lately, they've been invading the world of sports. There are now female jockeys, lady umpires, and some professional teams have half mockingly drafted female basketball and football players. To the best of my knowledge, nary a female behind has, as of yet, attempted to play professional baseball with the boys. But I can see the trend. As a matter of fact, these words will probably incite some crazed woman to break the all male barrier of major league baseball.

It will be a different game when the girls take the field. Oh sure, there will still be some Babes and Ruths, but most likely they will be a double play combination. And even if a girl comes sliding in spikes high, the fans will cry "Transexual!"

Stop thinking about the old, traditional baseball uniforms. Get ready for frills, mini-pants and the no-sweatshirt look.

There's the question of roommates on road trips. If the manager wants his catchers to sleep together and his outfielders to share the same room as some ballclubs do now, and one catcher's name is Mule Granite and the other catcher is Cindy Sensuous, the ballclub can expect a lot of letters from clergymen. Plenty of letters from the fans, too, when the catcher falls asleep at the plate in the next day's game. And can you imagine what will be discussed when Cindy Sensuous makes her way to the mound to talk things over with Clara Noseall? For example: Clara: "You must come over after the game for some apple strudel. I have the dreamiest new recipe. You take one pound of dark sugar and ..." Cindy: "Tell me later, Clara. Now keep the ball down low to Hog McSwine. He'll clobber anything up by his snout." Clara: "Oh, I'll get him out okay. Did you hear what he's been doing? He's been running around on the road trips while his sweet wife, Petunia, is home with the five kids."

Then, there are separate locker rooms and censored clubhouse discussions and different protective athletic devices. And I suppose they'll sit out their monthlies on the bench.

I may be missing the whole point of Women's Lib. All they want is equal opportunity. A ballclub could keep these ladies happy by providing them with a shot of whiskey, a plug of chewing tobacco and instructions to go out there and throw beanballs at their male counterparts.

On second thought, they should get a few girls to play with the Cubs. We wouldn't notice.

They gather in the locker room hours before game time. The men vary in age and background. The only thing they have in common is the knowledge they're the best in the business.

It's easy to spot the rookies. They pace back and forth, clearly showing their anxiety, dwelling on the day's game and what they have to do once they leave the sanctuary of the locker room.

The veterans, who've been through the Wrigley Field wars for many years, take things easier. They settle back, sip a beer and engage in casual conversation, waiting.

The boss man enters the room and with him, tension. Rookies and veterans alike lean forward in their seats waiting to hear names and assignments for the ballgame.

Then it comes. "Chipmunk, you take the cokes in the lower boxes down the right field line. The Roadrunner's got the beer in the left field grandstands. Eli, push the hot dogs in the upper deck. Newark, ice cream in the bleachers. Nate, take the peanuts behind home plate. Morgan, we're going to have to use you on popcorn today." On and on it goes until the last kid vendor draws his assignment and heads for the field with visions of becoming the next Al Morgan dancing in his head.

No feeling in the world compares with the one a young vendor gets when he first dons the faded blue overalls and slips the supporting belts around his shoulders. As he nervously walks to his position in the park, he goes over his lines. "Popcorn. You can't go wrong with popcorn. Popcorn. You can't go wrong with popcorn." or "Lemonade, made in the shade. Lemonade, made in the shade." For a minute he forgets the words and flushes, knowing that a failure such as this once the game starts could cost him two sales.

The good, young vendor doesn't sell his wares right away. If he is truly ambitious, he sits down and watches some of the all time great vendors go about their work, picking up pointers.

If he has sharp eyes, the young vendor will get a glimpse of the Roadrunner as he dashes by with a fresh load of beer. "Beer, who's next, who's next, beer, who's next, who's next?" he'll yell as he hands back change with one hand and pours a beer with the other. The Roadrunner is the all-time leading money winner on the vendor's tour.

The Chipmunk is one of the steadiest vendors on the tour. Chipmunk rarely has a bad day and has developed quite a personal following. Fans like to watch him froth at the mouth on hot days.

Newark is the Hoyt Wilhelm of the vendor's union. Although almost blind now, Newark has appeared at 48,392 consecutive games. He leads the league in frosty malts sold and is a particular favorite among the Bleacher Bums.

Nate is the top black star in the vendor world today. This amiable all star holds the single game record for peanuts. Nate shuffles from one aisle to the next singing, "ME AND MY PEANUTS."

The Babe Ruth of the vendor's league is the beloved Al Morgan. Morgan does not depend on tricky slogans or gimmicks to make his sales. He uses sheer ability. Morgan is a very versatile performer who is equally at home selling popcorn, Cokes, or ice cream. Morgan simply walks up to a fan, catches his eye, and says, "Popcorn?" His low key approach is a winner. Morgan has a great sense of timing. Precisely eight seconds after his last, "Popcorn?" he will repeat mysteriously, "Popcorn?" No one will ever forget the day Morgan was honored by some of his fans who presented him with a self portrait. Morgan modestly refused the picture, saying, "I got no place to put it. I come wit da bus."

The pessimistic newcomer to the vendor legion is discouraged by these stand-out performers. How could he ever approach the brilliance of these men? More important, how could he make a decent living in competition with these foxy salesmen?

The newcomer might have to turn to the Satellite tour. "If I really work," he says, "I can vend at Bozo's Circus and the Greyhound station downtown and at the Art Institute. Maybe someday I'll be making enough so I, too, will only have to work Cub and Sox park, the Stadium and Soldier Field."

Chances are this aggressive, eager young vendor won't make it. The latest stats show only one in every five peanut vendors make good, one in every seven pizza peddlers, and one in every ten beer men.

It's a tough field to crack, and even once you're an established veteran on the tour, there's only one Al Morgan, only one Chipmunk, and only one Roadrunner. The competition's tough in Wrigley Field — up there in the stands.

Randy Hundley, now a Cub coach, had the tenacity of the draft board after a hippie during his career as a Cub catcher. I recall a play at the plate when Randy almost lost consciousness following a collision. Although he was writhing on the ground in anguish, the ball which was riveted to Hundley's hand had to be removed with a blowtorch.

Hundley, who allegedly never utters a profane word, must have had trouble expressing himself in his pain. I've always wondered what he could be saying to the umpires when he barked at them in a violent manner for five minutes.

I assume it went like this: The bases are filled, two outs, and a full count on Hundley with the Cubs trailing by a run. Hundley takes a sweeping curve and starts to trot to first. "Steeerike three," yells the umpire. Hundley stops and turns on the umpire with fire in his eyes. The fans are screaming for the ump's blood. Hundley says to the man in blue, "Shucks, Ump. That was a plumb awful call."

Umpire: "Sorry Randy, it caught the corner."
Randy: "Fiddlesticks, it was low and away."
Umpire: "You didn't follow it all the way in, Randy."
Randy: "Confound it. That was ball four."
Umpire: "You'll get 'em next time. Now let's play ball."
Randy: "Wait just a pea-pickin' moment, you potato-head. You missed that pitch."

Umpire: "No, you missed it. Now let's play ball."

Randy: "You cock-eyed old bullfrog. I've got a mind to infest that wooden head of yours with termites."

Umpire: "Strike three, Hundley. Now get back in that dugout."

Randy: "Balderdash, you wishy-washy scarecrow. If you're a man you'll change your decision."

Umpire: "I couldn't do that if I wanted to. The other umps would get on me for changing my mind."

Randy: "Tough banana cakes, goll dang it."

Umpire: "THAT DID IT. YOU'RE OUT OF THE GAME!"

That's how a guy who never swears gets kicked out of a game.

Someone tried to make him swear once by asking him what movie was playing at a certain theatre (the movie happened to be *Village of the Damned*]. Supposedly he said, *Village of the you know what.*

Every year, hope springs eternal in the breast of a baseball fan. The die-hard fandom of all 26 major league teams secretly feels that, should their ballclub jell, they'd be the surprise team in the league. Through the summer, team after team goes by the wayside until only two remain. The hopes of millions of fans are shattered along the way.

Fans believing that their teams might be of championship fiber each spring should ask themselves two questions: 1. Is my team's overall speed above average? 2. Is the bullpen strong? If a fan can't answer yes with conviction to both of these queries, they would be better off supporting their local water polo team.

No one can point to a winner in the last few decades that didn't have more than adequate team speed. The teams that dominated in the 50's were the Brooklyn Dodgers and New York Yankees. Both are thought of as hard hitting ballclubs that won with power. Basically, this was true. But there was a vast difference between them and the Cincinnati ballclub of 1956. Cincinnati had power galore that season with flat-footed sluggers Ted Kluzewski, Gus Bell, Wally Post, and Ed Bailey. Great power ... no speed ... no pennant. The Dodgers also had flat-footed sluggers, but combined these power boys with speed merchants like Jackie Robinson, Junior Gilliam, Duke Snider. The Yankees had speed in Mickey Mantle, Phil Rizzuto, Gil McDougald.

Speed adds to the offense and is a big plus on defense. The sluggers have a hell of a time winning when a strong wind blows or a top pitcher is on his game. Every team needs a few men on their ballclub who might be able to steal a victory here and there. Unless a baseball fan can go down his starting lineup and find two or three men who can really move, he might as well not get his hopes up.

The bullpen can make a 20-game difference in a team's standings (remember Bruce Sutter?). You must have a superior bullpen. There has never been a world champion that did not get a great year out of one of their relievers. A strong bullpen can bail out a mediocre starting staff. Even if you have a fine starting rotation, they will look bad if they don't get help from the short relievers.

One of the hardest tasks is to evaluate a bullpen before the season starts. A big name reliever is prone to have a bad year periodically. It's happened to Sparky Lyle, Tug McGraw, Mike Marshall, Phil Regan, Ted Abernathy, and Lindy McDaniel. On the other hand, a relatively obscure pitcher can have a big year in the bullpen. It's difficult to be confident about your relief pitching. Generally, you can tell beforehand if it's bad. But you can't be sure it will be good.

One of the ways to get a handle on the bullpen ability of the current Cub team is to pay a visit to Rays Bleachers hot dog stand, the last stop before entering the house that Pete Whisenant built.

I have not been to a Cub game in the past ten years without stopping for a hot dog at Ray's. Those hot dogs with onions, relish, mustard, tomato, pickle and special seasoning salt will kill anything, even the butterflys in my stomach before the game.

Ray's is more than a place to grab a quick snack. It is a mecca for baseball talk. It is where you can get the inside dope. Last year, a shady-type character came up to me, complete with upturned collar and dark glasses, looked around, and then leaned over and whispered in my ear, "The Cubs have a kid in the minors who can throw better than Jenkins." I said, "Yeah, who is it?" This guy hissed, "Sh, Sh, Sh! Someone might hear ya. I can't tell you who it is, but his last name starts with an S." I tried to get more out of him, but he claimed he was a scout and couldn't divulge anything further. I told all my friends that Mr. S would soon appear and solve all the Cub pitching woes. Everyday one of them would call and ask where Mr. S was. Just as I was about to lose faith in the availability of inside information at Ray's, up from Wichita came Bruce Sutter.

The mysterious Mr. S had arrived.

Most Cub fans didn't do too well in school. If they had, they would have been Yankee or Red fans. But even if you're a Cub fan, try the following quiz anyway.

Match the names in the righthand column with the characteristic description on the left:

1. Intentionally tripped his mother and directed an obscene gesture towards her.	1. Harry Creighton
2. During a thunderstorm on an off day, forgot where he was and began interviewing the mailman.	2. Ernie Banks
3. While stranded on an expressway for two hours, exclaimed, "It's a beautiful day for a traffic jam."	3. Bruce Sutter
4. Saved three children from a raging fire, apprehended a notorious killer, and coaxed an escaped tiger back into his cage between three perfect innings.	4. Jack Brickhouse
5. Related to Vito Valentinetti.	5. Leo Durocher
6. Appeared on the mound once for the Cubs. The	6. Solly Drake

only guy he could get out was the pitching coach.	
7. Sold 42 loads of Cokes during doubleheader.	7. Name Any Outfielder
8. During a pitching change, snuck out to third base.	8. Philadelphia
9. Appeared on the mound often. The only guy he could get out was the pitching coach.	9. Larry Biittner
10. Dropped a routine fly ball in an important game.	10. The Chipmunk
11. This team frightens the Cubs even if we have a lead with three outs in the ninth.	11. Jose Cardenal
12. One of the fastest Cubs of all time.	12. Warren Hacker
13. Sold more H.A. hair arrangers than any other Cub announcer.	13. Vito Bopzinato
14. Slowest Cub of all time.	14. Peter Marshall
15. Utility man who should have worked for Commonwealth Edison instead of the Cubs (famous movie star named after him).	15. Butterfingers (or Snickers)

16. His son came to the Cubs with great potential, but not for baseball.

17. The candy bar named after Roy Smalley.

18. Hit three home runs and then was intentionally passed six straight times.

19. Picked the Cubs to win the pennant for past ten years.

20. Originated quotation "familiarity breeds contempt."

16. A Cub fan.

17. Al Gibson of Detroit Caesars (Slo-pitch softball)

18. Jimmy the Polack

19. Moe Thacker

20. Jimmy Stewart

SCORING*

15-20	Lock him up
10-15	Good, you get a cookie
5-10	Very good (really mediocre to bad, but most like the Cubs)
0-5	WHITE SOX FAN

*I'd be sued for libel if I put the answers in print. To find out how you did, meet me in the bleachers during the series. I'll be hawking books.

The greatest days at Wrigley Field are the worst. By 10:30 on the mornings of doubleheaders, all seats and standing room are often sold out. It hardly matters if the Cubs are playing Cincinnati, Houston or Poughkeepsie.

Last month, I got to Wrigley Field early but couldn't go in because I was holding tickets for Luigi, Smitty and Mox, and they were late. I told them I'd meet them by the balloon man in front of the ballpark. How'd I know his nephew was getting married that day? While I waited, I saw several sad scenes.

A birthday party group of ten youngsters and one mother arrived all aglow at the park around 11:30, one hour before game time. The kids all had their Cub hats and fielders gloves. But there were no tickets to be had.

An elderly couple got off the el after a long, tiring ride and walked the half block to the main gate only to learn their trip was fruitless.

I couldn't watch the misery anymore, so I moved on and waited for my friends at Ray's where I knew they'd eventually go. Two hot dogs later, we entered the park. People were hanging from the rafters.

It was a joyous occasion, except the Cubs got trounced 19-3 in game one. As you might imagine, the Cubs played swell.

Between games, I headed for the bathroom. So did 38,000 other people, all anxious to remove the beer from game one from their systems.

Naturally, there was a lot of pushing and shoving to get to the urinals. A basketball referee couldn't have called a violation for remaining in the same area for three seconds — we were going to the bathroom "on the fly."

Some people fell into an orbit whereby they entered the restroom and, before finding a spot at the urinal, were out the exit door. Back in the entrance line, a few even missed their second opportunity and ended up again on the wrong side of the restroom door. Some people fell into a trance and spent all of game two circling around and around. Luckily, this didn't happen to me, and I got back to my seat for the start of the second game.

The second game found the Cubs overtaking an early Montreal lead only to lose on a scratch Expo hit late in the game. I was enraged. The hapless Montreal Expos were derailing the Cubs' pennant express in the year we were finally going to make it. On the way home, I was devising all kinds of retribution for the Expos. The worst thing I could think of was forcing them to use the public restroom between games on doubleheader days.

My nephew, Mike, just turned eight and is burning up the Michigan City pee-wee league. He's actually only about one for eight, but that hit made the Michigan City newspapers. They reported his was the only hit made by the Sox (the team is aptly named) in a 17-0 loss. They misspelled his name, but he still expected to be stopped for autographs the moment he ventured out of the house.

Mike is really getting into baseball, so I took him and his ten year old sister Stephanie to Wrigley Field. Luigi had taken them to a Sox game the week before, and they were Sox leaners. If Luigi wasn't my friend, I'd press contributing to the delinquency of a minor charges against him.

We got into the car and Mike pulled out a Sox hat. Luigi's brainwashing was working. I hoped he hadn't turned Mike on to Beeman's chewing gum.

As soon as we arrived at the park, I grabbed ten all-star ballots and punched out all the Cubs names. I wrote in Roberto Pena's name. He hasn't been in the big leagues in ten years, but he is one of my all-time favorites. I'll never forget the opening day he drove in five runs for the opposition by his misplays at short.

We got to our seats. Michael was famished. I made him repeat the term CUB POWER ten times before ordering one of Oscar Mayer's finest. In truth, Cub Power is very similar to New York's Con Ed power this year ... non-existent.

While waiting for the game to begin, a young man dressed as a clown stopped when he saw the kids. "Mind if I sit in the aisle next to you?" he asked Stephanie. She said no, but I did. He was the most degenerate looking clown I had ever seen. "My name's Cookie. I'm a good friend of Ronald McDonald. In fact, this morning I stopped in a McDonald's and ordered a large coke and told them to charge it to Ronald's credit card."

I knew this guy was an imposter. McDonald's doesn't have any credit cards. I was about to ask him to move his big top and bottom out of there when he offered to give Stephanie a tulip. She said fine. He pulled a balloon out of his pocket and somehow transformed it into a tulip complete with a long stem. He then turned to me. "Can you buy me a beer? It's hot out here." I turned over 75 cents. If only the clowns on the Cubs had as much chutzpah.

The umpires picked that time to head for the conference at the plate. Why do four umpires born in South Carolina walk to the plate with their right wrists clasped in their left hands behind their backs looking like four orientals discussing the merits of the Wong Dynasty?

Michael wanted to know if there would be an umpire that pretends he's holding a pistol and shoots the runner when he's out at first. I told him no. I knew he was talking about Ron Luciano. He probably saw him at the Sox game and was enthralled. Luciano has almost made me an American League fan.

Mike wanted to know if the Cub scoreboard exploded when they hit a home run. I told him no.

He asked me where the light towers were. I explained there were none.

He got a hankering for Kentucky Fried Chicken, and I told him Wrigley Field has no chicken ... a few turkeys, but no chicken.

Things weren't going too well. The Cubs fell behind 4-0 early and kept pecking away until it was 4-1 in the bottom of the ninth. Michael yawned. Suddenly, the Cubs exploded. A missile to left, a hand grenade to right, a mortar shot to center and a home run bomb to win the game. Even Michael was excited. Stephanie was beside herself with joy.

We bought a Cub pennant and waved it out the window all the way home as we talked about the dramatic turnabout. We got to their house and both Michael and Stephanie thanked me.

As Michael was about to slam the door, he asked, "Who was Jungle Jim Rivera?" I slammed my head against the steering wheel.

I get frustrated when the TV cameras pan in on Herman Franks in the dugout. Why ... Herman is just sitting there, doing nothing and looking like just any fan watching the ballgame. Just sitting there. Doing nothing.

I am disappointed because I think managers should be managing. I mean, doing things. Giving signals. Calling on the phone to the bullpen. Getting excited. Getting mad. Figuring pitch by pitch, how to meet it, how to counter it, who to put in next, which righthander to put in should the other manager put in a righthander and who to send in his place later, in case the opposition should change their mind.

But Herman just sits there. Not managing. I feel cheated. Here I sit in front of my TV set, figuring, "What would I do if I were the manager?" and the real manager just sits there, doing nothing.

I feel like a kid at his first symphony concert, watching the conductor conduct and thinking that the orchestra could play every bit as well if that crazy guy wouldn't wave his arm at them. Now I think since Herman isn't doing anything anyway, why have a manager who gets all the money and the publicity and gets the public all riled up so they write letters to the Voice of the Grandstand and call WGN?

Let the Wrigleys fire Herman and get a new, active manager. One who paces up and down in the dugout and gives commands to the batboy and signals to the coaches and looks like he is thinking and gets excited and mad and smiles when things go right ... at least while the camera is on him.

It's a little-known fact that the Cubs set an all time major league attendance record last year. It's true that the number of people who paid to enter Wrigley Field did not surpass high season totals of many big league teams. But there were thousands of fans who didn't actually enter the park and still saw the games in person.

In every apartment building surrounding the field, hundreds of fans hang from windows and lie on rooftops watching the games. These people lounge arrogantly in (or on) their homes lapping up the sun in a haughty, cocky manner which says, "I'm watching this game for nothing, sucker. You paid to get in."

The fans in the boxes don't mind the cockiness of the apartment dwellers. After the game is over, they drive off to their suburban mansions. But the rest of us mind.

Actually, the people looking out of their apartment windows shouldn't be all that smug. While they're looking out at the ballgame for free, the 40,000 fans are staring in their windows. I mean, no one brings binoculars to the park to watch a silly ballgame.

All in all, it was a good season last year for the thrifty folks who chose the rooftops as their vantage point. Only three of them tumbled off the roof and two of them were insured.

One of them was showing a friend how Jerry Morales attempted a leaping catch. Another was demonstrating the proper way to make a head-first slide and alas, overslid the base. The third was not a baseball fan but had just seen a Superman rerun on TV and got carried away. They may not allow bottles or cans into the park, but they're sure in abundance on the rooftops.

Cub Fans' Pet Peeves

1. *Front Runner Fans*

Fans who show up at the ballpark only after a five game winning streak or as long as the Cubs are in first place. They're also very good at I-told-you-so's.

2. *Pessimists*

People who won't let you enjoy the rapture of the moment. Recently, George Mitterwald hit a two-run home run off Jon Matlack to give the Cubs a 2-1 lead in the seventh inning. I was screaming with delight when the phone rang. It was my mother, whose cautiousness taught me not to cheer too exuberantly when Superman saved Lois Lane. My mother told me, "Don't get too excited until it's over. If you cheer too soon, they'll lose." The Mets won 4-2.

3. *Impending Darkness Over Wrigley Field*

When there is an unusually long ballgame, or it's the second game of a doubleheader, Cub fans get preoccupied with the fading light. Fans don't want to come to a game to see a tie or a suspended game. In their hearts, they know it's a bit hazy and someone might not be able to get out of the way of a fast one inside. After an inning, when the four umpires converge to discuss what to do, fans hold their breath hoping for a reprieve ... one more inning.

4. *Cutting Away To Commercials at Precisely The Wrong Moment*

Just when a volatile pitcher is getting what he considers an unjustifiable hook from the manager, TV cuts away to an Oldsmobile commercial, missing the high drama of the angry, young man storming into the dugout, firing his glove against the wall and stalking off to the clubhouse.

5. *Finding Your Seats are Closer to the Washroom Than Home Plate*

I've sent away two months in advance for a Thursday afternoon game against San Diego and found my seats to be 30 rows up and down the line. You know no one else had the foresight to send that far in advance for tickets for this game. You also know that the men in the box office held back a huge block of premier tickets to be given only to those people who contribute to their Christmas fund. I wish Nixon would get back in power so all these guys can get their old jobs back.

6. *People Who Say the Cubs are Sunk if Sutter Hurts His Arm*

Cub fans have adopted my mother's philosophy and feel Bruce Sutter is too good to be true. He is the Messiah who will lead the team out of the wilderness. Every time he pitches they worry about his arm and hope he doesn't turn into a pumpkin during the pennant drive. They're out of their gourd.

One of the most exciting games ever played in Wrigley Field took place a few years ago. For almost an hour, thousands of fans stood on their feet shouting and pointing. It wasn't because the Cubs hit three grand slams. A huge fire erupted one and a half blocks away from the park and the flames and smoke shooting up in the air turned everyone's attention to the real action. Two apartment buildings were completely destroyed.

I was watching the game on TV, and the WGN camera crew spotted the flames in the second inning. Mr. Brickhouse was enthralled with the fire and consequently from time to time during the next three innings the viewers had to announce the game for themselves. The fire spread quickly and our courageous announcer was climbing into his asbestos suit when the firemen appeared.

Lloyd Pettit, the ex-WGNer whose only claim to fame was that he apparently didn't get along with Brickhouse, left the booth to get an on-the-scene report. Brickhouse kept assuring the audience that Pettit would be back soon. A few innings passed and Lloyd still wasn't back. I broke out in a cold sweat.

Pettit did come back to tell us that there actually was a fire, the cause unknown and fire chief something-or-other was there with 40 of his men. Always a fine report from Lloyd.

Meanwhile, on the field, the Cubs were using fire hoses as bats. Everything they hit were fluff balls. The Pirates, their foes for the day, definitely were more concerned about the fire than the Cubs. The late Bob Moose, the Pirate pitcher, had the Cubs looking like a box of Kleenex ... they popped up one after another. Moose shut out the Cubs 4-0. As a sportsman, I applauded him. As a Cub fan, I hated his guts.

For years, other teams have had Grab For Cash or Cow Milking contests in hopes of hearing the agreeable click of the turnstyles. The Cubs promoted green grass and fresh air. With the increased operating expenses facing major league teams (the ladies hawking Seven-Up behind the counters now demand $2.50/hr.), the break-even point has become one and one half million paying bodies through the gate. The Wrigleys have never been too interested in turning a profit in baseball, but they didn't want to pay to entertain Cub fans either. Gum sales have not been that brisk; the drug culture has more folks shooting up than popping Doublemint during moments of stress.

Consequently, the Cubs haven't given Barnum and Bailey any competition. No Sheboygan, Wisconsin Day or the flying Wallendas tightroping from the center field scoreboard to the pressbox. There has been a Bat Day and a Jacket Day and an Oldtimers Game. I bit for the Oldtimers Game and made a huge click as I entered the ballpark.

The game was between the Chicago Cub Oldtimers vs. the Hall of Famers. It was like wrestling. I wasn't sure if the game was for real or for fun. I didn't know whether to get worked up or not if the Cubs lost.

The players seemed serious enough. They all were in their old uniforms taking hitting and fielding practice before the game. The Hall of Famers in particular advanced to the plate eagerly to face the old Cub pitchers (Moe Drabowsky, the pride of Ozana, Poland, Dick Drott, Don Elston, Rich Nye, Milt Pappas, Phil Regan, Russ Meyer).

But was the game for real? Was that really Monte Irvin stumbling over the bullpen mound in left? Warren Spahn looked even balder than when he pitched for the Braves. Ralph Kiner was a lot slower or wasn't he hustling? Boudreau hadn't been kidding about starting the diet Monday. Was that soft pitch thrown by Rapid Robert Feller? Had these men gotten that old, that complacent? When Rich Nye retired Kiner and the Cubs took the lead, I really thought the game was fixed.

Then Beckert booted a ground ball and Santo popped up, angrily tossing his bat aside, and I began to see some normalcy.

But the Hall of Famers couldn't capitalize on Cub mistakes. It was as if they didn't care. They had proven themselves. Meanwhile, the Cubs were playing with a dogged fervor.

Phil Cavaretta was stretching every which way for errant throws. Of course, Phil always had desire. I remember Cavaretta at 38 finishing his career with the White Sox scoring from second on a single to tie a game with a belly flop slide. The fans gave him a standing ovation, and I, being a nine year old, could not understand what was so great about a man scoring from second on a single. Beckert was replaced by Popovich who handled everything in sight. Jerry Kindall and Stan Hack at short and third played like men possessed. Moose Moryn, Bob Will and Andy Pafko patrolled the outfield as never before. Even J. C. Martin made contact at the plate.

My Cubs defeated the men with the bronze busts in Cooperstown. It seems possible that the Cubs are like French wine, getting better with age. Maybe we should field more 50 year olds.

CUB IMAGES

Billy Williams' sweet swing ...

Lou Brock's rookie year and the fear and agony on his face as he chased a misjudged ball back to the vines ...

A roundhouse curve ball thrown for a strike by Sad Sam (Toothpick) Jones ...

Hearing Jack Brickhouse's "Oh, brother" after a late inning home run by the opposition ...

Ernie Banks' fingers "playing the piano" on his bat handle ...

Moose Moryn crashing into the right field wall padding ...

Ken Hubbs fluidly gobbling up a grounder and flipping it to first ...

Ron Santo clicking his heels in 1969 ...

Hank Sauer collecting packets of chewing tobacco along the left field vines after hitting a home run ...

Jose Cardenal feigning advancement from third to home ...

Watching a Willie Mays' home run off Cal Koonce bounce down Kenmore Avenue ...

The fans yelling olé olé the day Adolfo Phillips hit four home runs ...

Warren Hacker, Paul Minner, Johnny Klippstein, Glen Hobbie, Howie Pollet, etc., making the long walk from the mound to the dugout after a rough inning ...

Don Kessinger with his "boarding house reach" taking away a base hit ...

Dee Fondy legging out a drag bunt ...

Sam Taylor chasing a wild pitch thrown by Dick Drott back to the screen ...

Tony Taylor genuflecting before stepping into the batter's box ...

Watching the bullpen crew jump for cover on a smash hit down the line ...

Milt Pappas complaining about his lost perfect game ...

Pat Pieper's predictable line-up presentation ...

Don Elston's sidearm delivery ...

Frankie Baumholtz catching every ball hit to the outfield between Hank Sauer and Ralph Kiner ...

Gene Baker, his body contours forming a C, in his batting crouch ...

A mid-week afternoon game played in ugly weather in front of 985 fans during the low years ...

Big Bob Rush's high kick and homerun-or-nothing swing ...

Hal Jeffcoat amusing the pre-game fans by kicking his hat onto his head from the centerfield ground...

Jack Brickhouse incessantly using his hands as he explains another defeat ...

The yellow numerals on the scoreboard indicating runs scored during the inning in progress ...

Hank Aaron striking out on a Lindy McDaniel forkball that bounced in front of the plate ...

Hank Aaron letting two of Bob Anderson's fastballs go by for strikes before hitting a grand slam ...

The brown colored vines early in the season ...

George Altman's stiff armed swing ...

The depressing games back total in the standings for the past 32 years ...

The biggest loss of the Cubs' 1977 season may be to chewing gum. Of the 10,000 shares of stock which comprise the legal makeup of the Cubs, over 8,000 shares are held by the William Wrigley family. Of the remaining shares held by the public, most, if not all, are held by fanatical Cub fans who are obviously not in it for the money. Shares rarely reach the marketplace, and when they do the price fluctuates wildly from one trade to the next. The last two times the stock was traded the price went from $485.00 (during spring training) to $750.00 (when the team was 25 games over .500).

The recent death of Phillip K. Wrigley and shortly thereafter of his widow, Helen, has produced a most difficult situation for the rest of the family. Phillip Wrigley was reported to be worth over $100,000,000.00 at his death. The bulk of that wealth was comprised of stock holdings in the Cubs and in the Wrigley Chewing Gum Company. The Internal Revenue Service and the State of Illinois are anxious to receive their fair share of the estates, and lo and behold, the Wrigley family is cash poor like all the rest of us. Since the Chewing Gum Company usually makes money and the Cubs usually lose money, the family may be forced to sell off their interest in the Cubs, unless they can devise a way to raise the money needed to pay taxes.

There are some ways out. Cub management could trade Bobby Murcer to Oakland for a ten percent share of the I.R.S. bill and a player to be named later. Or Cubs' tickets could be printed on the outside wrapper of Juicy Fruit Gum, thereby producing an extra 17 cents (the cost of the gum) for the family each time a ticket was sold. And the fans could always pass a collection plate at each game throughout the stands and thus raise enough money to pay the taxes.

The alternatives are unthinkable for Cub fans. To sell the club would mean the end of the benevolent and passive leadership the Wrigley family has made us come to know and love. Cub fans do not want a self-made hamburger for an owner or a guitar playing cowboy.

The Wrigley family, while it has not produced a winner for its fans for some time, has endeared itself to the fans nonetheless. After all, it was Phillip Wrigley who decided that 22,000 seats should go on sale on the day of the game so that anyone could come and see a game if the mood struck them that morning. It was Wrigley who refused to install lights so that all games have to be played during the day when the kids could see them. And it was Wrigley who kept the price of the tickets as low or lower than any other team in baseball. The Cubs have also never had a significant holdout problem because of the fairness with which the Cub owner operated in contract negotiations.

Chicago sports fans have had many mercenary professional sports owners forced upon them. The fans have suffered from the money-hungry, fans-be-damned attitude of these civic leaders.

A great man with compassion like the late Cub owner Phil Wrigley was sometimes less appreciated by the fans than he should have been. Fans have a general mistrust for the league of sports owners, so rather than bombarding Wrigley with superlatives, they merely accepted him as an OK guy.

Durocher said that nice guys don't win, but he was wrong. The Lip created more dissension on the Cubs than any other time in my tenure as a fan, and he didn't win. We have more reason than ever to win now. It would be a hell of a tribute to the old man.

Last year, after making my own dinners for too long (always pizza ... pizzeria pizza, frozen pizza, home made pizza), and after years of squiring a few lovelies and lots of uglies to places I didn't want to go to (Joffrey Ballet, Stuttgart Ballet, Trenton Ballet), I met and married Diane, who performs all her wifely duties in a most satisfying way.

This year she presented me with my son, Danny. Danny is a delight, a future second baseman. Nobody spits up like my son.

I have moved to a suburb of Chicago near an expressway system that will whisk me downtown, catapult me to work, or eject me onto the Indiana dunes.

When not writing, I earn a decent livelihood by implanting thoughts of catastrophies into the minds of insurance prospects.

I'm in good health.

I improved my bowling average by seven pins last season.

But until the Chicago Cubs run roughshod over the baseball world, my life is incomplete.

My life has never been easy. Like when I was an infant and couldn't get my arm thru the pajama sleeve or later at the beach when a wave always destroyed the sand creation I had just completed.

Too often I have prepared a bowl of Rice Krispies, complete with sugar and apricot slices, then gone to the refrigerator to find the only liquid in there was Mountain Dew.

In school, when I was the only kid who knew Louis XIV's castle was at Versailles, the teacher never called on me.

And when I got to adulthood ... not getting to the window in time and the horse paid $22.40 to win. Racing to the airport to meet the plane of a very special person and hearing the plunk-plunk of a flat tire. Salivating for a T-bone steak and finding out the restaurant specialized in seafood.

But nobody knows the trouble a Cub fan has seen. We have gone through 32 years of frustration. Thirty two years of seeing the New York Mets win or the Baltimore Orioles (the old St. Louis Browns) or the Oakland A's (the former Kansas City A's) or who ever.

Please. It is now time. I'll be happy to suffer one year of reaching for the toilet paper and finding an empty spool in trade for the championship that would make my life complete.

Cubs All-Time Roster Since The Last Pennant

	Major League Record or Average	*Years with Cubs*
Abernathy, Ted	63-69	1965-66, 1969-70
Aberson, Clifford	.251	1947-49
Adams, Bobby	.269	1957-59
Adams, Charles ("Red")	0-1	1946
Addis, Robert	.281	1952-53
Adkins, Dewey	2-4	1949
Aquirre, Henry	75-72	1969-70
Aker, Jack	47-45	1972-73
Alexander, Matt	.141	1973-74
Altman, George	.269	1959-62, 1965-67
Amalfitano, Joseph	.244	1964-67
Amor, Vicent	1-3	1955
Anderson, Bob	34-46	1957-62
Andre, John	0-1	1955
Arcia, Jose	.215	1968
Ashburn, Richie	.308	1960-61
Aspromonte, Kenneth	.249	1963
Atwell, Maurice ("Toby")	.260	1952-53
Averill, Earl	.242	1959-60
Baczewski, Fred	17-10	1953
Bailey, Edgar	.256	1965
Baker, Gene	.265	1953-57
Baker, Thomas	0-1	1963
Balsamo, Anthony	0-1	1962
Banks, Ernie	.274	1953 71
Barber, Turner	.289	1917-22
Barber, Stephen	121-106	1970
Barragan, Facundo ("Cuno")	.202	1961-63
Bauers, Russell	31-30	1946
Baumann, Frank	45-38	1965

Baumholtz, Frank	.293	1949, 1951-55
Becker, Heinz	.263	1943, 1945-46
Beckert, Glenn	.283	1965-73
Bertell, Dick	.250	1960-65, 1967
Biittner, Larry	.268	1976
Bilko, Stephen	.249	1954
Bithorn, Hiram	34-31	1942-43, 1946
Bladt, Richard	.215	1969
Block, Seymour ("Cy")	.302	1942, 1945-46
Bobb, Randy	.100	1968-69
Boccabella, John	.219	1963-68
Bolger, Jim	.229	1955, 1957-58
Bonham, Bill	43-57	1971-76
Borkowski, Robert	.251	1950-51
Boros, Stephen	.245	1963
Borowy, Henry	108-82	1945-48
Bouchee, Edward	.265	1960-61
Bourque, Pat	.215	1971-73
Breeden, Danny	.151	1971
Breeden, Harold	.243	1971
Brewer, James	69-65	1960-63
Briggs, Johnny	9-11	1956-58
Bright, Harry	.255	1965
Brinkoph, Leon	.182	1952
Brock, Lou	.296	1961-64
Broglio, Ernest	177-74	1964-66
Brosnan, James	55-47	1954-58
Brown, Jophery	0-0	1968
Brown, Tommy	.241	1952-53
Browne, Byron	.236	1965-67
Bryant, Don	.220	1966
Buhl, Bob	166-132	1962-66
Burdette, Freddie	1-0	1962-64
Burdette, Lew	203-144	1964-65
Burgess, Forrest ("Smoky")	.295	1949, 1951
Burke, Leo	.239	1963-65
Burris, Ray	34-29	1973-74

Burton, Ellis	.216	1963-65
Burwell, Richard	0-0	1960-61
Buzhardt, John	71-96	1958-59
Callison, Johnny	.264	1969-71
Calmus, Richard	3-1	1967
Campbell, Joseph	.000	1967
Campbell, Ronald	.247	1964-66
Cannizzaro, Chris	.235	1971
Cardenal, Jose	.277	1972-76
Carlsen, Donald	2-4	1948
Cardwell, Don	102-138	1960-62
Carpenter, Robert	25-20	1947
Carty, Rico	.308	1973
Cavarretta, Phil	.293	1934-53
Ceccarelli, Arthur	9-18	1959-60
Chambers, Clifford	48-53	1948
Chipman, Robert	51-46	1944-49
Chiti, Harry	.238	1950-56
Christopher, Lloyd	.243	1945
Church, Emory	36-37	1953-55
Church, Leonard	0-1	1966
Clemmons, Douglas	.229	1964-65
Cline, Ty	.238	1966
Coggins, Frank	.215	1972
Cohen, Hyman	0-0	1955
Colborn, James	61-62	1969-71
Cole, David	6-18	1954
Coleman, Joe	133-131	1976
Collum, Jack	32-28	1957
Comellas, Jorge	0-2	1945
Compton, Clint	0-0	1972
Connors, Bill	0-2	1966
Connors, Kevin ("Chuck")	.238	1951
Cooper, Mort	128-75	1949
Cooper, Walker	.285	1954-55
Cosman, James	2-0	1970
Covington, Wes	.279	1966

Cowan, Billy	.236	1963-64
Cross, Joffre	.162	1948
Culler, Richard	.244	1948
Culp, Ray	122-101	1967
Curtis, Jack	14-19	1961-62
Cusick, John	.174	1951
Dallessandro, Dominic	.267	1940-47
Dark, Alvin	.289	1958-59
Davis, Bryshear	.260	1970-71
Davis, James	24-26	1954-56
Davis, Thomas	.294	1970,72
Day, Charles	.256	1970
Decker, George	36-43	1969-72
Del Greco, Robert	.229	1957
Dettore, Tom	8-11	1974
Distaso, Alec	0-0	1969
Dobernic, Jess	7-3	1948-49
Donnelly, Edward	8-12	1959
Dowling, Dave	1-0	1966
Drabowsky, Moe	88-105	1956-60
Drake, Samuel	.153	1960-61
Drake, Solomon	.232	1956
Drott, Dick	27-46	1957-61
Dubiel, Walter	45-53	1949-52
Dunnegan, James	0-2	1970
Dunn, Ron	.241	1974
Eaddy, Donald	.000	1959
Early, Arnie	12-20	1966
Edwards, Bruce	.256	1951-54
Edwards, Henry	.280	1949-50
Elia, Lee	.203	1968
Ellis, James	1-1	1967
Ellsworth, Dick	115-137	1958-66
Elston, Don	49-54	1953, 1957-64
Erickson, Paul	37-48	1941-48
Ernaga, Frank	.279	1957-58
Estrada, Chuck	50-44	1966

Fanning, William	.170	1954-57
Fanzone, Carmen	.224	1971-74
Fast, Darcy	0-1	1968
Faul, Bill	12-16	1965-66
Fear, Luvern	0-0	1952
Felske, John	.135	1968
Fernandez, Frank	.199	1971-72
Flavin, John	0-1	1964
Fleming, Leslie	16-21	1942-46
Fodge, Gene	1-1	1958
Fondy, Dee	.283	1951-57
Frailing, Ken	10-16	1974
Freeman, Hershell	.143	1958
Freeman, Mark	3-3	1960
Freese, George	.257	1961
Frey, Linus	.269	1937, 1947
Friend, Owen	.227	1955-56
Gabler, William	.000	1958
Gabrielson, Len	.253	1964-65
Gagliano, Phil	.238	1970
Gamble, Oscar	.256	1969
Garagiola, Joe	.257	1953-54
Gardner, Richard	14-18	1967
Garman, Mike	14-16	1976
Garrett, Adrian	.185	1970,1973-74
Garriott, Cecil	.000	1946
Gerard, David	2-3	1962
Gerberman, George	0-0	1962
Gernert, Richard	.254	1960
Gigon, Norm	.171	1967
Gilbert, Charles	.229	1941-43.1946
Glossop, Al	.209	1946
Goetz, John	0-0	1960
Goryl, Johnny	.225	1957-59
Grabarkewitz, Billy	.236	1974
Grammas, Alex	.247	1962-63
Gregory, Leroy	0-0	1964

Gura, Larry	19-16	1970-73
Gustine, Frank	.265	1949
Haas, Eddie	.243	1957
Hack, Stan	.301	1932-47
Hacker, Warren	62-89	1948-57
Hairston, Johnny	.250	1969
Hall, Jimmie	.254	1969-70
Hamner, Ralph	8-20	1947-49
Hands, Bill	111-110	1966-72
Hamilton, Steve	40-31	1972
Hanyzewski, Edward	12-13	1942-46
Hardin, William	.143	1952
Harris, Vic	.217	1974
Hartenstein, Charles	17-17	1965-68
Hatten, Joseph	65-49	1951-52
Hatton, Grady	.253	1960
Heath, William	.236	1969
Hegan, James	.228	1960
Heist, Alfred	.255	1960-61
Hendley, Robert	48-52	1965-67
Hendricks, Elrod	.219	1972
Henry, William	46-50	1958-59
Hermanski, Eugene	.272	1951-53
Hernandez, Ramon	23-14	1968
Herrnstein, John	.220	1966
Hiatt, Jack	.251	1970
Hickman, Jim	.252	1968-73
Hiller, Frank	30-32	1950-51
Hillman, Dave	21-37	1955-59
Hiser, Gene	.202	1971-74
Hoak, Donald	.265	1956
Hobbie, Glen	62-81	1957-64
Hoeft, Billy	97-101	1965-66
Holtzman, Ken	165-135	1965-71
Hooton, Burt	63-66	1971-74
Howe, Calbin	0-0	1952
Hubbs, Ken	.247	1961-63

Hughes, James	15-13	1956
Hughes, Terry	.209	1970
Humphreys, Robert	27-21	1965
Hundley, Randy	.236	1966-73
Hutson, Herb	0-2	1974
Irvin, Monford	.293	1956
Jackson, Larry	194-183	1963-66
Jackson, Louis	.213	1958-59
Jackson, Ransom	.261	1950-55
Jacobs, Tony	0-0	1948
Jaeckel, Paul	1-0	1964
James, Cleo	.228	1970-71,1973
James, Richard	0-1	1967
Jeffcoat, Harold	.253,39-37	1948-55
Jenkins, Ferguson	203-150	1966-73
Jimenez, Manuel	.272	1969
Johnson, Benjamin	2-1	1959-60
Johnson, Donald	.268	1943-48
Johnson, Kenneth	91-106	1969
Johnson, Louis	.258	1960-68
Johnson, Richard	.000	1958
Jones, Clarence	.248	1967-68
Jones, Samuel	102-101	1955-56
Jones, Sheldon	54-57	1953
Jurges, William	.258	1931-38, 46-47
Kaiser, Donald	6-15	1955-57
Kelleher, Mick	.205	1976
Kellert, Frank	.231	1956
Kelly, Robert	12-18	1951-53
Keough, Marty	.242	1966
Kessinger, Don	.254	1964-74
Kindall, Gerald	.213	1956-58, 60-61
Kiner, Ralph	.279	1953-54
King, Charles	.247	1958-59
King, James	.240	1955-56
Kitsos, Christopher	.000	1954
Klippstein, John	101-118	1950-54

Knowles, Darold	56-63	1976
Koonce, Calvin	47-49	1962-67
Kremmel, Jim	0-4	1974
Krug, Chris	.192	1965-66
Krukow, Mike	0-0	1976
Kuenn, Harvey	.303	1965-66
Kush, Emil	21-12	1941-42, 46-49
LaCock, Peter	.221	1972-74
Lade, Doyle	25-29	1946-50
Lamabe, John	33-41	1968
Landrith, Hobert	.233	1956
Landrum, Don	.234	1962-65
LaRoche, David	29-23	1973-74
LaRose, Victor	.000	1968
Larsen, Donald	81-91	1967
LaRussa, Tony	.199	1973
Lary, Al	.250	1954-55, 62
Lee, Don	40-44	1966
Lee, William	169-157	1934-43, 47
LeMay, Richard	3-8	1963
Lemonds, David	4-8	1969
Lennon, Robert	.165	1957
Leonard, Emil	191-181	1949-53
Littlefield, Dick	33-54	1957
Littrell, Jack	.204	1957
Livingston, Thompson	.238	1943, 45-47
Locker, Robert	57-39	1973
Long, Dale	.267	1957-59
Lown, Omar ("Turk")	55-61	1951-54, 56-58
Lowrey, Harry ("Peanuts")	.273	1942-43, 45-49
Lundstedt, Thomas	.092	1973-74
Lynch, Matt	.286	1948
Mack, Raymond	.232	1947
Madden, Clarence	.248	1946, 48-49
Madlock, Bill	.337	1974-76
Madrid, Salvador	.125	1947
Manville, Richard	0-0	1952

Marquez, Gonzalo	.235	1973-74
Marquez, Louis	.182	1954
Marshall, James	.242	1958-59
Martin, J.C.	.222	1970-72
Martin, Morris	38-34	1959
Massa, Gordon	.412	1957-58
Mathews, Nelson	.223	1960-63
Mauch, Gene	.239	1948-49
Mauro, Carmen	.231	1948, 50-51
Mayer, Edward	.217	1957-58
McAnany, James	.253	1961-62
McCall, Robert	4-13	1948
McCullough, Clyde	.252	1940-43, 46-48 1953-56
McDaniel, Lyndall	141-119	1963-65
McGinn, Dan	15-30	1972
McKnight, James	.231	1960,62
McLish, Calvin	92-92	1949,51
McMath, Jimmy	.143	1968
Meers, Russell	3-3	1941, 46-47
Merriman, Lloyd	.242	1955
Merullo, Leonard	.240	1941-47
Metkovich, George	.261	1953
Metzger, Roger	.233	1970
Meyer, Russell	94-73	1946-48,56
Mickelson, Ed	.081	1957
Mickelsen, Peter	45-40	1967-68
Miksis, Edward	.236	1951-56
Miller, John	4-6	1947
Miller, Robert	69-81	1970-71
Minner, Paul	69-84	1950-56
Mitterwald, George	.235	1974
Moisan, William	0-0	1953
Monday, Rick	.267	1972-76
Montreuil, Al	.091	1972
Moore, Donnie	0-0	1976
Morales, Jerry	.264	1974-76

Morehead, Seth	5-19	1959-60
Morgan, Robert	.233	1957-58
Morgan, Vernon	.225	1954-55
Morhardt, Meredith ("Moe")	.206	1961-62
Moryn, Walter	.266	1956-60
Muncrief, Robert	80-82	1949
Murphy, Daniel	.177, 4-4	1960-62
Myers, Richard	.000	1956
Neeman, Cal	.224	1957-60
Nen, Richard	.224	1968
Newman, Ray	3-3	1971
Nichols, Dolan	0-4	1958
Nicholson, William	.268	1939-48
Niekro, Joe	68-75	1967-69
Noren, Irving	.275	1959-60
Norman, Fred	64-64	1964, 66-67
North, Bill	.270	1971-72
Northey, Ronald	.275	1950,52
Nottebart, Donald	36-51	1969
Novotney, Ralph	.269	1949
Nye, Richard	26-31	1966-69
Oliver, Gene	.246	1968-69
Oliver, Nate	.226	1969
Olsen, Vernon	30-26	1939-42,46
O'Neill, Emmet	15-26	1946
Ortiz, Jose	.301	1971
Ostrowski, John	.234	1943-46
Ott, William	.304	1962,64
Owen, Arnold ("Mickey")	.255	1949-51
Pafko, Andrew	.285	1943-51
Pappas, Milt	209-164	1970-73
Passeau, Claude	162-150	1939-47
Paul, Mike	.115	1973-74
Pawelek, Ted	.250	1946
Pena, Roberto	.245	1965-66
Pepitone, Joe	.258	1970-73
Perkowski, Harry	33-40	1955

Phillips, Adolpho	.247	1966-69
Phillips, Taylor	16-22	1958-59
Phoebus, Tom	56-52	1972
Piktuzis, George	0-0	1956
Pina, Horacio	23-23	1974
Pizarro, Juan	131-105	1970-73
Plummer, William	.194	1968
Poholsky, Thomas	.171	1957
Pollet, Howard	131-116	1953-55
Popovich, Paul	.233	1964,66-67 1969-73
Porterfield, Bob	87-97	1959
Pramesa, Johnny	.268	1952
Prim, Raymond	22-21	1943,45-46
Prince, Donald	0-0	1962
Pyecha, John	0-1	1954
Qualls, Jimmy	.223	1969
Radatz, Richard	52-43	1967
Ramazotti, Robert	.230	1949-53
Ramsdell, Willie	24-39	1952
Ranew, Merritt	.247	1963-64
Raudmann, Robert	.200	1966-67
Reberger, Frank	14-15	1968
Regan, Phil	96-81	1968-72
Reich, Herman	.279	1949
Renko, Steve	76-93	1976
Reuschel, Paul	5-5	1976
Reuschel, Rick	62-64	1972-76
Reynolds, Archie	0-8	1968-70
Rice, Del	.237	1960
Rice, Harold	.260	1954
Richards, Fred	.296	1951
Rickert, Marvin	.247	1942,46-47
Roach, Melvin	.239	1961
Roberts, Robin	286-245	1966
Robertson, Daryl	.105	1962
Robertson, Donald	.000	1954

Rodgers, Andre	.249	1961-64
Rodriguez, Fernando	0-0	1958
Rodriguez, Roberto	4-3	1970
Rogell, Billy	.267	1940
Rosello, David	.234	1972-76
Ross, Gary	23-43	1968-69
Roznovsky, Victor	.218	1964-65
Rudolph, Ken	.211	1969-73
Rush, Robert	127-152	1948-57
Santo, Ron	.277	1960-73
Sauer, Hank	.266	1949-55
Savage, Ted	.233	1967-68
Sawatski, Carl	.242	1948,50,53
Schaffer, Jimmie	.223	1963-64
Schaffernoth, Joseph	3-8	1959-61
Scheffing, Robert	.263	1941-42,46-50
Schenz, Henry	.247	1946-49
Schmidt, Fred	13-11	1947
Schmitz, John	93-114	1941-42,46-51
Schramka, Paul	.000	1953
Schroll, Albert	6-9	1960
Schult, Arthur	.264	1959-60
Schultz, Barney	20-20	1961-63
Schultz, Buddy	3-1	1976
Schultz, Robert	9-13	1951-53
Schurr, Wayne	0-0	1964
Scott, Richard	0-0	1964
Secory, Frank	.228	1944-46
Selma, Dick	42-54	1969
Serena, William	.251	1949-54
Shamsky, Art	.253	1972
Shantz, Robert	119-99	1964
Shaw, Robert	108-98	1967
Silvera, Charles	.282	1957
Simmons, Curtis	193-183	1966-67
Simpson, Thomas	1-2	1953
Singleton, Elmer	11-17	1957-59

Skidmore, Roe	.1000	1970
Slaughter, Sterling	2-4	1964
Sloat, Dwain	0-1	1949
Smalley, Roy	.227	1948-53
Smith, Bobby Gene	.243	1962
Smith, Charles	.239	1969
Smith, Paul	.270	1958
Smith, Robert W.	4-4	1959
Smith, Willie	.248	1968-70
Solis, Marcelino	3-3	1958
Solomon, Eddie	1-1	1975
Spangler, Al	.262	1967-71
Speake, Bob	.223	1955,57
Sperring, Rob	.221	1974
Spring, Jack	12-5	1964
Steevens, Morris	0-2	1962
Stelmaszek, Dick	.170	1974
Stephenson, Chester	4-5	1971
Stephenson, John	.216	1967-68
Stewart, James	.237	1963-67
Stone, Steve	40-48	1974
Stoneman, Bill	54-85	1967-68
Stringer, Louis	.242	1941-42, 46
Sturgeon, Robert	.257	1940-42,46-47
Summers, Champ	.207	1976
Sutter, Bruce	6-3	1976
Swisher, Steve	.223	1974-76
Talbot, Dale	.247	1953-54
Tanner, Chuck	.261	1957-58
Tappe, Elvin	.207	1954-56,58,60 1962
Tappe, Theodore	.259	1955
Taylor, Sammy	.245	1958-62
Taylor, Tony	.261	1958-60
Terwilliger, Wayne	.240	1949-51
Thacker, Morris	.177	1958, 60-62
Thomas, Frank	.266	1960-61, 66

Thomas, LeRoy	.255	1966-67
Thompson, Robert	.270	1958-59
Thornton, Andre	.253	1973-74
Thorpe, Robert	0-0	1955
Tiefenauer, Bobby	9-25	1968
Todd, Jim	7-8	1974
Tompkins, Ron	0-2	1971
Torres, Hector	.211	1971
Toth, Paul	9-12	1962-64
Tremel, William	4-2	1954-56
Trillo, Manny	.241	1976
Tyrone, James	.180	1972,74
Upham, John	.308	1967-68
Usher, Robert	.235	1952
Valentinetti, Vito	13-14	1956-57
Vander Meer, John	119-121	1950
Varga, Andrew	0-0	1950-51
Verban, Emil	.272	1948-50
Voiselle, William	74-84	1950
Wade, Benjamin	19-17	1948
Wade, Gale	.133	1955-56
Waitkus, Edward	.285	1941,46-48
Walker, Albert	.227	1948-51
Walker, Harry	.296	1949
Wallis, Joe	.259	1976
Walls, Lee	.262	1957-59
Ward, Chris	.203	1972,74
Ward, Preston	.253	1950,53
Warner, Jack	0-2	1962-65
Warwick, Carl	.248	1966
Whisenant, Peter	.224	1956
White, Elder	.151	1962
Wilhelm, Hoyt	143-122	1970
Will, Bob	.247	1957-58,60-63
Williams, Billy	.290	1959-74
Williams, Dewey	.233	1944-47
Willis, James	2-2	1953-54

Winceniak, Edward	.209	1956-57
Wise, Casey	.175	1957
Woods, Jim	.207	1957
Wright, Melvin	2-4	1960-61
Wyse, Henry	79-70	1942-47
Young, Don	.218	1965,69
Zamora, Oscar	13-14	1974
Zick, Robert	0-0	1954
Zimmer, Donald	.235	1960-61

About the Author

The truth best be known. The author of this book is as convoluted as some of the thoughts contained in the vignettes. He was born in Chicago, Illinois in 1946 and raised in Hyde Park. His secondary education was just that. He somehow managed to graduate from Southern Illinois University with a degree in Journalism, even though he spent most of his time following his classmate, Clyde Frazier (now with the New York Knicks), around the campus.

While some of the material included in this book is the figment of his fertile imagination (the latter being a prerequisite for being a Cub fan), most of the stories really happened. He still has his bandaged transistor radio and he still checks the wind when he wakes up each morning. This season, however, he hopes the wind is coming from the north at 60 miles per hour.

He has worked as a reporter, factory worker, encyclopedia salesman, shoe salesman, vendor, claims adjuster, and is presently an owner of Skyway Insurance Agency. He is also a member of the Illinois Athletic Board.

He is wild about pizza, his wife and his newborn son, Danny. He is not so wild about the White Sox, Brickhouse and a Cub loss.

Typeset by
Roth Studios, Inc.
426 South Clinton Street / Chicago 60607
(312) 431-0681